Smartr Living:

Rough Draft Edition

A manuscript written by and for someone who thinks jobs are bullsh*t.

ISBN-13: 978-1532727627

ISBN-10: 1532727623

Table of Contents

Introduction
What is Smartr Living?

I had one of those "aha" moments this morning... one of those famous "criddle" moments that ends in me writing a book, or at least starting on a new one. I have written a whole lot more than I have published at this point. Once a project gets to the proofreading and editing part, I send my writing off to my editor, and soon start a new project – regardless of what it is. I get so wound up in this cycle, that I often have piles and piles of unfinished projects.

Having too many unfinished project has led to a revolutionary idea, that I will call – The Rough Draft Edition. Creating a Better Edition of Breaking Point sounded so much better than calling it a second edition. And since I believe the publishing game is changing for the better, it's about time to stop worrying about perfection so much, and just worry about getting my content out there.

Though, on top of the rough draft thing, my "aha" moment this morning should alleviate some of the foggy-headedness I have been feeling the last few months. I have been so focused on testing The Smartr App (reaching perfection) that I have not made much time for anything else in my life. But today, I decided to kick a little ass, and get the universe working for me again. A new paradigm. A new day. My project – The Smartr App – is launching like any second; so here I am, writing a book about the bull shit that led up to this moment. And it is going to be a good day.

Funny to think about the "ups and downs" of my life – which when I think about it now, has always been constant. I seem to have these cycles that continue to repeat. Seasons of situations which seem to place success so near to my fingertips... just to fall out of reach shortly thereafter. The difference between now and then, is I realize I was the problem in the past. The only reason why success fell out of reach before is because I was lazy enough to allow it to slip away. Maybe this is all because I had not yet realized the "smartr" way to do things.

There is no clear definition for "smartr." After all, it is just a word. That I figured would make for an easier trademark. But in all seriousness, for the first time in my life, I spelled something wrong, and didn't get in trouble for it. I walked away from perfection. I created something from my vision... my humor... my skewed perception of the world – and once again, I witnessed one idea, leading to the next idea, and to the next. Who know removing the letter "e" from that word would be one of the best things to ever happen to my life?

It may be funny to some, me saying "life" and all. But that is what being an entrepreneur is all about. Employees will never understand the abuse a real entrepreneur will endure – just to see a vision through to completion. Not many people will ever know what it is like to publish 20 books before selling any copies. Not many people will know what it's like to starve your way through an almost 2 year long custody case, just so you can continue paying for the attorneys. Not many people will know what it is like to have the determination to build a company which will truly change the world. Does this make me better than anyone? Hell yes it does.

People always say, "I wouldn't change a thing about my past." And I think to myself, "I could change a million things about yesterday alone." But that is life. The only thing that really matter is growth. Evolution. Becoming smarter. Better. Figuring out a way to live a more prosperous, and spiritually fulfilling life. I said earlier... does this make me better than anyone? Yes. It makes ME better. Better than the person I was yesterday. And you know what? I don't give a shit if it's perfect either. I am growing anyway.

Before I go much further...

This book is going to be a mix of a few different manuscripts. In 2015, I had 6 or so major hardcover projects that fell victim to my "writing without editing" projects pile – but I figure, the only way for you to truly understand this book, is to understand some of the spiritual journey I had do undertake to get here. So I have to include a bit from "The God Theory." – A book which is more or less about the journey I believe all men go through, once they are ready to become God after this life.

Not many people would understand the "Project Trillionaire" philosophy I came up with; my idea of how one can build a million, billion, or trillion-dollar company in a lifetime:

1. Don't give up, or give a shit.
2. Do it for God/the world.
3. Build something huge, and give it all away.

Building a sixty thousand dollar a year company takes a lot longer than building a billion dollar company. Do you know why? Selfishness. Greed. Obviously the person trying to make sixty grand a year, or even a hundred grand, or a million a year is not thinking big enough. Sixty thousand dollars doesn't do much in this world. Neither does a million. And it sure as hell won't change much of anything.

Yes, if you want to get big things done, you have to have big dreams, and be willing to take big steps. And if you really want to build a trillion-dollar company, you have to do it by giving the trillion dollars back to everyone who helped you build it. However, I think in order to understand all of what I am trying to stay... you have to understand a little more about my vision. My purpose. What I know I am here to do. I had my first near life experience a few years ago, and it changed every single moment of my life from that point on.

I remember my first "near life" experience.

About 6 months or so prior, I was working out at my apartment gym with a client of mine in the early hours of the morning. We were working on shoulders, and I was doing my duty of spotting and motivating him. I eventually got to the point to where I would work out with my clients as well, rather than just standing alongside them. This kept them motivated even more so and I got to gym it up multiple times a day, which allowed me to get in better shape faster. At the time, I was dating a girl and we were going through a very stressful time as she was not used to dating a single father, and I had just quit my corporate job to start my own training business. Not only was money tight, but she was used to going out with her friends throughout the week and on the weekends and it was a big change when I would have to work late evenings and spent 3 to 4 days a week with my little girl.

For some reason, stress perhaps, my heart had been feeling a bit weird for a few days. Painful more than weird. I had these moments where I would get winded or need to sit down, and these moments did not take place when I was working out, they were completely random and came on without warning. Sometimes hurt more than others, but being the stubborn man I was, I just decided to not only ignore it, but tell no one about it when it happened.

This particular morning, I was completely out of it. My heart was hurting so bad that I could not concentrate on anything. My client continued to ask me if I was ok, at which point I would lie to him and tell him I was, and we would go back to working out. I walked back to the water fountain because my room temperature water bottle had just run out, and took a huge gulp of the ice cold water which came from the spout. I felt that surge of cold running down through my chest that you feel when your throat is dry and you are dehydrated... then I collapsed to the floor in pain.

My client ran over to me and said he was going to run out to his car to get his phone and call 911. I was hearing about every other word as I grabbed my chest and arm in pain, and managed to tell him that we needed to get back to the apartment before my girlfriend went to work. I laid down in the backseat while he sped back to the apartment. He helped me walk upstairs and there she was in the bathroom, getting her hair ready. I rested up against the wall in the hallway and said, "Babe, we need to go to the hospital, now."

For a moment, it almost seemed as if she thought I was kidding. She looked at me with a very peculiar look on her face and said, "Are you serious? What is wrong?"

I said, "I don't know," and slid to the floor. "I think I am having a heart attack."

Over the course of the next few months, I spent many days and many nights in hospitals. I was given multiple beta-blockers and blood pressure medications... in various doses and combinations to see what work. I spent most of my time hooked up to halter monitors so hospitals and doctors miles away from me could monitor my heart throughout those days and nights. My life completely changed in an instance, and I felt like it was slipping away from me with each passing day. I became humbled, quiet, and wanted nothing more than to be a better father. In that time, we even took a trip to the west coast to a few beautiful cities I had never visited before, and I got to take my first ambulance ride from our hotel in downtown Seattle to a cardiovascular hospital in Cherryville, Washington.

So many days bouncing around from hospital to hospital to getting in more debt than I could have possibly imagined. I met doctors who made guesses about what was wrong, and doctors who had no clue that would prescribe me pain medications and discharge me without an and examination or explanation. I learned that some doctors come in contact with certain illnesses and ailments, and if you are not lucky enough to run across one of those doctors, you may not be taken seriously. All I could do to help myself was carry around a folder with all of my medical records inside it.

I finally bit the bullet and went to a state funded hospital back home. I had heard so many horror stories about it that I was almost scared to walk in the door. I decided if I felt like passing out again, I would take a chance. That day came very soon.

I was laying in the emergency room when a doctor came in after multiple series of tests and told me he was at a loss on what to do. He did however show me some graphs and give me a breakdown of what was going on with my heart. He said my resting heartrate was about 50bpm since I had spent some time getting in shape, but at any moment's notice, by heartrate would jump to 130+ bpm without warning. Since I spent a significant amount of my life obese, this was not really affecting me as my resting heartrate was already so high... I was actually completely unaware it was going on. Being "healthier" now, I was feeling it, and the shock to my nervous system was overbearing. He did tell me that a Neurocardiologist would be coming to the hospital the following morning to look me over and let me know what kind of medications they would send me home with. He came in the following morning and said, "Hello Mr. Criddle, we are going to prep you for surgery."

The things that happen when our eyes are closed...

I have never been a fan of hospitals, even though I felt very safe anytime I was in a hospital at this point. I spent a lot of time telling friends and family members to go home and they didn't have to be there with me since I was sure they had better things to do. I did not let my daughter see me much in these times because I knew she would not understand and I didn't want her to absorb the stressed energy of others in that environment and grow worried over something that did not make sense to her. On the day of the surgery, I found out they were going to cauterize parts of my heart to try and fix whatever electrical problem was going on with me. Luckily it was not open heart surgery, I had the luxury of them sending tools through major arteries in my groin rather than cutting open my chest. Everyone cries when you are being wheeled out of the prep room... I remember that from having my tonsils taken out as a small kid and my parents being overly worried. The prep nurse looked back and said, "Don't worry, he will be back."

I have never been a fan of sedation either. To me, it feels like sleeping without dreaming and being aware of everything that is going on within your surroundings without feeling anything. You can feel your body move and shift. You can feel nerve endings being manipulated by chemicals and doing their duty of not allowing certain signals to be fed to your brain and sensed as pain, but you are still aware of the communication going on. You can hear doctors and nurses even though they sound like the adults on Charlie Brown cartoons... and if you listen closely enough, you can hear nothing else. Complete and utter stillness and silence within the space of time and action while professionals go to work on your body. Since I had been sedated a few times in my life, I thought this would be what dying felt like... it was not.

Before I went under, I told the doctor that I was going to need an above average dose of medication to keep me under, and I also told them they may want to strap me down because I was going to wake up fighting. She laughed a little and I expressed my seriousness since it had happened to me on every occasion prior. When I opened my eyes and came to, it was like being reborn again. The lights were too bright and voices were too loud. I did not want to be on the table and began throwing my arms and fists in every direction to get up. The doctor that performed the surgery was a fairly large man, and he laid across my torso as they strapped my legs down, (my legs had to lay flat to keep the wounds closed) and two different nurses grabbed my arms. Someone kept forcing my shoulders down onto the table, and what kept sounding like "mmhhmm mmm mmhm mmm," finally turned to, "Calm down Jason. Jason, calm down."

My mom later explained to me, that when they wheeled me back to my room after recovery, there was a man in the bed next to mine... and any time he spoke, my body would react in fear and I kept screaming for my father to leave me alone. I remember this, but I do not remember it – if that makes any sense. I was drugged up and I felt groggy and out of place during this time, but it eventually wore off – my mom told me she cried while this was happening.

The next couple of days I just sat in silence. Throughout this ordeal that took months, I refused pain medication. I was always told I was one of the hospital's best patients because I was always so calm and never asked anyone for anything. They took blood from me so many times that the veins in my arms and hands were no longer available for use, so they began taking samples from my feet. As they took blood every couple of hours, I had no regular sleep patterns. I was not one to watch TV, so I spent my time looking out the window. The silence in my head still existed. There was no longer an assortment of random chatter; the only things I could hear were the thoughts I wanted in there. The silence became loud.

Even though the surgery "fixed" the problem, my heart rate continued to increase randomly. The doctors told me this may happen, and he also told me that since I had grown so used to feeling pain in my chest, that anxiety may eventually onset at the anticipation of feeling pain, which would indeed cause pain that felt like the original problem. Since my alarms would go off anytime my heartrate would jump, the nurses eventually turned the audible alarms off so I could sleep. The silence in my mind grew louder, the pain was still present, and my awareness of my body and self would grow with every passing moment. I lost track of time and I felt the person I used to be slowly slipping away from me. As I type this, I realize how little sense it makes... oh how words can sometimes not describe what we are wanting to explain. The best words I can use are, while I wanted so much to see my daughter, I also wanted to die... almost as if I was being urged by a greater part of me to let go.

One of those nights, I got a new nurse, or at least thought I got a new nurse. Thinking back at the events of what transpired, she could have very well been a figment of my imagination, or sent by someone in a much higher place of understanding than I was at the time. She came in and asked if I was getting any rest and wrapped my arm in a sleeve to check my blood pressure. She performed the standard protocol that nurses and techs usually did; look at my chart, look at the monitors hooked up to me and the monitor she brought in. She came over to my IV and said she would bring me a new bag soon; she was just going to empty the remaining saline solution into me so I could get an influx of fluids. She pressed a few buttons hooked up to the apparatus and walked out the door, turning off the lights on the way. I had this sudden memory pop into my head of there being magnesium sulfate in one of the bags hooked up to me as well, and then the thought disappeared. I felt one of those quiet moments of stillness, and my body became hot. Everything seemed out of place as I looked up at the bag of magnesium sulfate quickly rush down the tube and into my veins. Every inch of my being was now overly warm, I closed my eyes, and let go.

I got up from the bed without any wires hooked up to me... no IV and no pain. My body did not feel right; it did not even feel like a body. I looked towards the door which seemed to be a few miles away and began making steps towards it, then blinked. When I blinked, I saw, heard, felt, smelled, sensed, and became everything. It was almost like those old TVs with the "snow" broadcast coming through because there was nothing set on that particular channel. Even though there was nothing on my channel, I became everything. The "blink" seemed to take minutes, then my eyes opened. I turned around and looked at my bed, and I saw my lifeless self, laying there with everything still hooked up to me. I looked at the monitor and saw a brief flat line begin to take place. All I thought to myself was, "I need to get out the door to let my nurse know I have died."

I turned back towards the door and blinked again. I saw the future and the past. I saw stars, planets, distant galaxies, light, light, and more light. I felt enormous and so small. I understood what my life and everyone else's life was meant for, then my eyes opened again.

I continued to walk towards the door again with my mission hard set in me now. I had to get to the door and tell the nurse to come and check on me as I was still laying lifeless in my bed. I blinked again and heard my own voice exclaim, "Its ok Jason. You don't have to go back if you don't want to." I wanted to. I wanted to be a father... it was the only thing holding me back. All I wanted to do was experience this divine moment of unexplainable beauty, knowing, stillness, and bliss. My eyes opened, and I was closer to the door.

I had more moments of blinking, or glimpsing rather. My mind turned into this antenna of sorts. During each blink, I felt as if millions of years of information were being downloaded into my being and becoming part of my thoughts and consciousness. I began realizing how every single fraction of every molecule in the world is in synch with everything and everyone in the universe. Every action I would take and every single thought I would ever think affected the entirety of both time and space throughout the cosmos. I continued to take steps towards the door and in between the steps were more series of glimpses. I felt so alive. The only way I could explain it is to say I felt like God. I felt like I created the universe and created my "self" and my own awareness of my "self." I was right at the door now, reaching out with my hand and heard one last time, "Jason, you don't have to go back."

I touched the door handle and awoke on my bed, screaming as the nurses came rushing in. The lights flipped on and the light was so blinding. I did not know how I had ever lived with such a false pretense of this wavelength which had been explained to me throughout my life as being called "light." I experienced light for the first time and it was not "this." My body was still warm, but the heat was dissipating. I was so relieved at the thought of being able to be a father, but I was so disheartened at the fact that I did not let go… that I did not stay in the realm of pristine beauty and understanding. The decision to come back, while a necessary one, felt like this life was an unrealistic bad dream. I had finally been awakened to what we really are… what God is, what the universe is, and what we are all supposed to do and become. I did not just see my purpose, I understood the covenant; the agreement I made when I decided to create my "self" and my own awareness before coming to this plain of existence and matter. Everything that was and always will be channeled through my being, and slowly started to slip away as the noise and chatter of my conscious mind began to come in. I finally had an understanding of all of the bullshit we are told and made to believe which holds our minds and hearts at bay – which in turn keeps us from the understanding that we really are God. I was turning to a human "doing" once again. I had a brief experience of living as a human "being" for the first time in this existence.

You are God.

I am not saying you should change the way you begin introducing yourself to people you have just met… but it is time you realize the power within you. The reason you picked up this book is because your path has led you to looking over these many pages of text at this very moment in your life. This book is what you need to transition into the next phase of spirituality the universe has mapped out for you. You made an agreement with yourself before coming to this plain of existence; a covenant. Your divine higher self has been calling you to fulfill the purpose you have forgotten about for far too long, and that purpose is far greater today than it has been these past few days and months. All of the decisions you have made your entire life have led you up to this very moment, especially, your most recent. This is your moment of transcendence.

Your moment of letting go. Your moment of becoming the person you are meant to be.

The egocentric God we were raised to believe has never existed. God is true love. God is the power of creation you feel whenever you cry for help, when you first meet a loved one, or when your children come to you with a problem that brings out withheld emotions that allow you to let go and come into true love. God created you to experience the universe through your eyes and your mind. You are the true love you have sought for over these many years. You picked up this book because that very truth revealed itself to you. So, now, here we are.

On a journey together to become the most powerful beings the cosmos has ever witnessed. We will learn the importance of patience, forgiveness, compassion, manifestation, spirituality, love, and the very essence of elements which will cause us to soar. On this walk beset before us, your questions of significance will be answered time and time again. You will have to promise me though; you will let go of your ego. You will not allow judgments and paradigms of hate and fear cause you to question your soul which is screaming and begging for mercy and change of the self. You have had far too many moments of not being able to life with your "self." Those moments end today.

You are all of the love you need. God is witnessing his creation through your eyes. You are abundance. You are the heaven you are seeking. You are pure bliss, abundance, and everlasting wonderment. I praise you for your change. I praise you for your decisions to become one with our creator and your new found life. I praise you because you are God. I love you because you have taught me to love.

"Some time ago." – Tirthraj Vyas

So, where were we? Oh yes. Projects. Books.

For the last couple of years, I have been pumping out content, with complete disregard for whether or not the world needed it. When I wrote my first book, I wrote a book that I wanted to write. I never thought to myself that I needed to be writing a book that someone would want to read. I brushed up on my marketing skills, built a publishing company to help other authors grow, thinking it would help me build my name as an author as well. I sold a few extra copies because of that move, but nothing extravagant ever happened. I definitely would not have call myself a successful author because of it.

Even the publishing company was a problem. Even though I could see the value in becoming an author as an entrepreneur, I never realized how much work it would be to sit down and actually ghost write and edit a book with another author until I actually did it. I ended up in further in debt than when I started. Of course, this led to "smartr" thinking once I realized I could hire other authors and editors – and have everyone work together in a collaborative effort in order to get things done quicker. Alas, having a book for yourself is still a commodity, and not some sort of necessity to the average person.

My investment firm had not done much of anything since firing the old partner and changing the way we were doing business. I had been taking time to fly out to meetings and do the hand shaking bit to stay alive in the game, but it's also a corrupted industry. There are plenty of great entrepreneurs with wonderful ideas, but any money exchanging hands all comes down to relationships. I have tried to help hundreds of entrepreneurs since being in this game, and the few I have been able to give genuine help to did not receive any sort of funding because of their business model. They only received the funding because I was able to introduce them to the right person at the right time – and that person just so happened to take their head out of their ass, and invest in something that day. I'm not slamming any particular investors... I am slamming the game.

Writing is fun, but it only pays the bills when books are selling. Which takes me going out and speaking in front of people. Which takes this, and this, and that. But I don't want to be a "writer." Or be known for being a writer. Or be known for being a speaker... especially a motivational speaker. I would rather be known for being the guy who saved the entire planet, he just happened to write hundreds of books in the process.

It's funny to think about all of the books I have on the market, and have had on the market for some time. Quite a few have become best sellers... and most have not sold a copy. Why? Because, what the heck am I doing right now that would condone anyone catching my name and buying one of my books? Then I think about the authors I have helped with my publishing company who are upset when their books do not sell any copies either. Well, what are you doing with your life? You are a plumber... a chiropractor... I am just a writer and an entrepreneur. Sure I have been on the news a few times, but I was also doing something worthwhile at the time.

Sure, I am about to launch The Smartr App... and it is going to change the entire planet, but no one else really knows what I have been doing with my time. It's not like I am playing the role of the unsuccessful guy, telling other people how to be successful – like a few of the new internet sensations that are sniffing out easy dollars from social media drones.

I want to start directing movies as well. And spending more times focused on illustrated works and cartoons... but I don't want to be known as a director. Or be known JUST for making a lot of awesome content... I would rather be known for being the guy who saved the entire planet, he just happened to make great freaking content at the same time.

I never wanted to be known for having a huge publishing company, or having a successful financial firm.

I never wanted to be known for changing oil, or being able to check the fluid levels of a car faster than anyone in my bay.

I never wanted to be the fastest sandwich maker the owner of our franchise had ever seen when I was 15 and working at Subway.

I never wanted to be a great cashier, promoted to assistant grocery manager, after sacking groceries for just 2 hours – and being called, "ambitious."

I never wanted to be chosen to build a pool company for a home builder – because I was already known for building a successful pool company.

I never wanted people to give me high-fives because I could make their lawn look better than their last landscaper.

I never wanted to be the guy who could make multilevel marketing look easy... or teach people to be better at sales.

I never wanted to build gas-powered RC cars, or collect Star Wars toys. I never wanted to have 20 snakes and be a really good snake handler. I never wanted to gain an interest in half the shit I have done. I have never wanted to work any of the jobs I have worked. I have always said, "a man should fear being successful at something which does not matter." And frankly, now I just think jobs are bullshit. It's all part of the game of life which is built and run by the people who understand the monetary system. There is really nothing special about it.

I have always wanted to do something spectacular. It wasn't until the last few years when I finally started realizing what money actual was – what value means – how the human mind works. Behavior, faith, ambition, honesty… all of these character traits come along with the struggle of success. And being successful is absolutely necessary if you intend to change the lives of seven billion people who do not yet know your name.

I never let a lack of sales or not reaching some oblong expectation get in the way of creating something though. If I want to make a cd or dvd, I make one. If I want to write a book, I write it. If I want to start a company, I start it. That doesn't mean I am always "successful," or that the world is ready for it, but I do it anyway.

I never understood just how crucial failure was in climbing the ladder to success. And I can tell you one thing above all else… I have become really good at failing. A strength any and all can adapt is being able to change one's mind. There are a lot of times when an idea will not work. You have to adapt, or change pace all together – and finally move on if necessary. But so many are afraid to do so. We are conditioned to never quit… but quitting, like many other traits, is necessary for growth too. How many people will go 5, 10, or a lifetime worth of years with the same mindset, values, mentality, etc…? if you wish to evolve in this life whatsoever, you have to be able to work out every possible scenario which could lead to failure, long before you ever let failure get ahead of you. The only competition you really have in this life is yourself, and frankly, some of us are just too damn ignorant and unwilling to change.

With Smartr Pills, I thought I had the answer. I had spent so long helping other people make money in network marketing, it only made sense for me to start my own network marketing company. With as many seminars I had put on – as many promotors I had spoken with – to be the *evangelist (Greg would call it) of my own MLM company – now this made sense. Maybe this could be my "big thing."

When I was a personal trainer, I had helped hundreds of people lose weight with my natural supplement formulas and combinations. And the brain supplement I had developed for my own use after I left the training industry is still top notch in my book. Hell, I would like to think it has something to do with all I have accomplished... but I digress.

I thought the word "Smartr" was the most genius thing I had come up with in a long time. Plus, up until this point, no one had yet turned a brain supplement into a network marketing company. All the pieces kept lining up... including the couple of investors I got to believe in the project. I found 3 different manufactures to start my project once I had a minimum amount of orders. I already had the team in place to build my website to get the project launched. All I really needed was a strong database, server, and a genealogy structure to tie it all together.

Once I shopped around and found out the software to run my company was going to cost me $35,000 dollars, it was like being kicked in the nuts. I sure as hell didn't have $35,000 dollars lying around... and that wasn't even product costs. Before I knew it, my company that had managed to raise $10,000 – after only spending $500 to get started, was crashing. I knew I had to find a different solution. This was a problem that couldn't be solved.

Thinking back

I remember sitting down last year and starting another writing project; I had this idea – that anyone could raise $10,000 for just about any business model in a very short amount of time. I have learned that angel investors are a certain type of person, and scheduled investors are another. Both have their own perspectives and ways of doing business. Both are useful to your cause... you just have to learn the difference between the two. I will go into investor personalities in other publications, but for now, just keep in mind that people make investment decisions from a business mindset, as well as a personal mindset. Stay away from people who take things personally. They become headaches – more so than they could ever be "helpful" investors.

In the time I ran Legacy Status Investments, I ran across so many people who would tell us they needed a million dollars for their marketing campaign. I would tell them, "first, you don't need a million dollars of marketing money; you need sales and someone willing to sell. Second, you need a product that sells itself."

There are very few people that need a million dollars to get any business off the ground. Investors usually invest in projects that don't need money. Just like banks typically loan money to people who do not need loans. Concepts do not raise funds nowadays, and (un)fortunately for me, I am a visionary. I have a tendency to share a pretty great story with some people... but that doesn't mean I can keep the virgin investor who takes business personally, in "check."

I learned in network marketing... you may be good at selling a kit or a membership or autoship, but you are not going to be there to resell that person month after month. If your product, service, or message does not have unquestioned value, it is doubtful the sales will continue to be made.

The same rules stay in play when it comes to building a real business on investor dollars. You may get them to write a check up front... but that doesn't mean their enthusiasm will remain with you and your vision month after month after month. It doesn't matter how hard your struggle may be, no one will ever understand turmoil the way you do. Yes, I am talking to you.

It's funny how quickly a dream can crumble if you allow it to crumble... We had already spent our investor dollars on marketing materials and a temporary ecommerce system for our customers. We had commitments from a couple of, what I would have called "big time" (big talk) investors – who were not putting any ink on checks. I had raised that $10,000 that I felt the need to write a book about, and I had nothing to deliver. Why? Because I never wanted to become successful at creating a brain supplement multilevel marketing company. Anything I was going to do at this point had to be beyond some stupid network marketing company.

What the hell am I going to do?

Pray. Meditate.
Whatever the heck you want to call it.

I pace. Do you pace?

Well, I do. I pace when I think. I pace when I talk on the phone. I pace long before I realize I am pacing.

I remember having a talk with my step son about affirmations. I was telling him, the President of these United States does not have to walk around telling people he is the President. They just know it.

Michael Jordan will never have to introduce himself as Michael Jordan. Bill gates does not wake up in the morning and look himself in the mirror and shout out loud, "I am a billionaire!"

It's unnecessary. And somewhere along the way, I allowed my ego to get in the way, and I became content with the same house, and the same car – all over again. Thinking that just because my bills were being paid, I was a billionaire.

Then reality hit... because our software wasn't finished... and the bills were not paid. I was the author of 20+ books, the owner and operator/investor of dozens of businesses, a speaker that pissed people off a whole lot more than he motivated them – id been on multiple radio shows about parenting, behavior, nutrition, finances; and now I have $400 in the bank and some change.

Regardless of what I think I may have accomplished... I still have people relying on me to pay the bills. I am sweating as errors continue to pour in from my developers. It seems like something is always in the way of me getting this app launched. After all, of all the bullshit ideas I have ever had, I finally designed a company that could change the world. Little did I know, the only thing standing in the way of the app being fixed, was just a little bit of faith.

I knew God had delivered me this vision. I knew this company was going to be the first domino in a string of dominoes that would change the world. Then I thought of writing this book. I thought of what content I had lying around. I thought of what value I could offer my readers. I thought about the company I designed that would change lifestyles and business alike. And the only thing that made sense, was to sit down and write a book. Not only write a book, but write a book on faith. And remember what I came here to do.

Take a moment to pray. Take a moment to think. Take a moment to meditate. Take a moment to create something spectacular.

In the last few months, I have done a lot of things. I have created some new books... and I built a business that will change the way people live –

but I have not taken a whole lot of time to pray. The only reason I experienced that original "aha" moment is because my life was crashing down on me once again.

The only difference this time, is I decided I was not going to let circumstances control me. I was not going to – once again – allow other people's decisions to influence my future or my desires or the things I wanted for myself or my family.

Once I discovered the so-called "secrets" to the universe, I made a goal to make a million dollars. I was 30 then, and I "thought" by the time I became a 31-year-old man, I would be a millionaire. 31 came and went, and instead of giving up... I decided that the only reason I did not reach my goal is because my goal was too small; so I decided that by the time I became 32 years old, I would become a billionaire.

My 32nd birthday came and went... and instead of giving up, I realized – I am a fucking man of God. I have a purpose and that purpose will be fulfilled. I did not become a millionaire, because millions were not enough to fulfill my desires. There are not enough millions to help me accomplish my tasks needed to create peace on earth.

I did not become a billionaire, because billions were not enough to fulfill my desires. There are not enough billions on the planet to help me accomplish the tasks needed to create peace on earth.

I decided on the day that I started on the book that you are reading right now, that I AM a Trillionaire. Yes, I thought about it a few times. I created a book about it. I created a concept apparel company about it. But it wasn't until April 1st of 2016, that I decided and knew – I am going to be a fucking Trillionaire. And I am going to do it NOW.

All I needed to do was take a moment out of my day to pray. All I needed to do, was think about Today. Today is an affirmation... a prayer I wrote some time ago. You will notice I placed it at the end of every single chapter. My hope is – by the time you get to the end of this book, you will be able to not only remember the prayer, but you will also be able to focus on today.

Today.

Today, I am thankful... for each and every day. I will be better every day. I will do more every day. I will greet each day with laughter, love, and gratitude, and say goodnight with a brief reflection of the day's events before I honor my creator for the gift of today. This day was given to me, and should not be taken for granted. I need to concentrate on living in the now, but I will momentarily reflect on the day's events for the sole purpose of seeing what I can improve upon before the sun rises tomorrow and my eyes close tonight. When given the choice to do nothing and take action, I will forever choose to take action. The person who used to do nothing is gone. If this person reappears, I will become aware, take action against them, forgive myself, and move on. TODAY, I TAKE ACTION.

Today, I will become wiser. I will choose to absorb knowledge and educate myself in every subject matter possible, as my thirst for wisdom is a primary driver in my success and freedom. I will condition my body and eternal spirit to make peace with the only enemy I thought I had... my mind. I have spent far too long fighting what I thought was a never ending battle, but not anymore. It is impossible to defeat an enemy that only exists within me. I have no enemies... I have no failures... only opportunities for growth and expansion. TODAY, I GROW. TODAY, I EXPAND. TODAY, I AM WISER.

Today, I will win. Tomorrow I will win. For the rest of my life, I will win. I will be successful. I will be great. My rewards and wealth are a byproduct of the value and service I offer those around me, including myself. The lives I change are my true reward... My success is a byproduct of the lives I change, as well as my decision to change myself. My life is my reward. TODAY, I AM SUCCESSFUL. TODAY, I AM GREAT. TODAY, I WIN.

Today, I overcome. I shall suffer no longer. I will not waste my energy on long-term goals. I will break my long-term goals down into simple daily steps, and instead, devote my energy to becoming the person I must become to reach my long-term goals. Yesterday, I was not that person. Today, I am that person. I am stronger than yesterday; mentally, physically, emotionally, and spiritually. I have not only adapted to, but have overcome the thief that robbed me of fulfilling my destiny yesterday... my mind. TODAY, I AM STRONGER. TODAY, I OVERCOME.

Today, there is no enemy. Today, there is no fear. Not anymore. I am the only thing that has ever stopped me, but today, I forgive myself. I forgive everyone I feel has ever done me wrong, simply because, no one has ever done me wrong. At the time they performed actions which I thought were against me, or wrong, I did not understand myself the way I do now. I can show them compassion, pray for their healing, and hope one day we can sit side by side while I share with them how grateful I am for every breath they take. TODAY, I FORGIVE.

Today, I un-focus. Sometimes people will focus their anger towards me, but I will not focus my anger towards them. I am in control of my feelings, my emotions, and my actions. Only I can make the choice to become upset or angry, and I no longer make that choice. I forgive them. I forgive myself. Pain is necessary, but my suffering is optional. Today I make the decision to never suffer again. TODAY, I AM IN CONTROL.

Today, I realize my purpose. My body belongs to me and so does my mind. And now, I am now in control. This magnificent and beautiful vessel was created for one thing and one thing only... my purpose that God has given me. My destiny that I now realize. It is said that the two most important days of our lives are the day we are born, and the day we realize WHY we were born. For me, that day is today. TODAY, I AM MY PURPOSE.

Today, I make the decision to be wealthy. I make the decision to be healthy. I make the decision to be successful. I make the decision to have a smile on my face even when no one else is smiling. I make the decision to provide for those who cannot provide for themselves. I make the decision to stay in control of my mind. I make the decision to forgive even when I am not forgiven. Today is my purpose. Today is my gift. Today, I am in control. TODAY, IS MY GIFT. TODAY, I TAKE RESPONSIBILITY FOR MY LIFE.

Today, God will move mountains for me, because today, I will move mountains for God. TODAY, I AM READY.

Chapter 1
You can be whatever you want to be, and make a lot of money doing it.

It is a pretty amazing time we live in. For the first time in history, or at least the history we have been taught... mankind does not necessarily need a "job" for survival any longer. You can truly make a living just being you. You don't need titles, certifications, or a degree. You just need passion in something, and belief in yourself.

Much greed and many wars ago, our civilization was introduced to the Industrialized Revolution – which, somewhere along the way, helped to destroy the American dream. We began building companies based on a corporate structure, which was taught to us – not beneficial. We created factories and assembly lines, and allowed unions and everyday workers to both exploit and fall victim to a lifestyle that broke apart the family and destroyed the environment, more so than it ever helped the world progress. Mass production, over consumption, and throwing away everything became a mindset; built for 1 generation of people – the baby-boomers.

We started designing things that would break, so we could replace them later with more things that break. Why fix a toaster when you can buy a new one? Why fix a marriage when you can "buy" a new one? Our mentality to over-consume and throw away has now become the way we approach all of life – relationships, our children, our homes, and pets.

Now we look for cheap deals, immediate gratification, and value has all but disappeared. People have been forced to make decisions based on the greater good of the dollar, rather than the greater good of themselves or their well-being.

Fortunately, I see a change on the horizon. It seems Corporate America is losing the battle they picked with us so long ago. For the first time in our lives, entrepreneurs are appearing in droves. The recession which forced so many people out of work caused a ripple in time and space that no one expected to happen. What is it you ask? People started figuring out – jobs are bullshit. And they are unnecessary. If you won't give us a means to make a living, we will sure as hell find one on our own.

Lowest price is bullshit. The same as minimum wage, and "benefits." We are coming into a new age... and I even developed The Smartr App because I could see it coming. It seems to me, the only thing that makes sense – if the middle class wants to survive, and our Government is unable to help, we need to find our own way to thrive. The companies we have been buying things from for so long can share profits with their customers. People can make their own livings by doing whatever they want, as well as representing the brands they use the most. All they need is a system to get them there.

Could you imagine living in a world where Nike provides your clothes, Walmart provides you with food and living needs, while Nissan gives you a discounted car? And even if these companies were not paying for everything, what if they were contributing a few hundred, or even a thousand dollars a month to your bottom line? Most people just need basic living expenses taken care of. If our Government wants to help, they should be doing it be providing people with "jobs." And those "jobs" should be building green and sustainable infrastructure to replace the old crap we have that is still contributing to old problems; but that is a talk for another book.

Emma and I still go on walks... and many mornings and middays, I see our neighbors out with their families, or tending to their lawns. And the simple fact that I have the pleasure of witnessing this at 2pm on a Tuesday afternoon further reinforces the change I see coming. People are beginning to realize that time and freedom are far more important that vacations and benefits. Like I already said, the only thing they really need, is some basic living expenses taken care of. And for those who realize they don't need a car for every driver in the home – and for those who are not ashamed to move back home while they build a real life for themselves – life is becoming even sweeter.

This is why The Smartr App was born. Even though I had always loved the simple idea of a compensation structure with a network marketing company... it dawned on me that most people just can't or wouldn't be willing to make a living selling protein or makeup. Some will, but most won't. And helping some people realize they can have all the time and freedom they want to obtain, by simply passing around a shopping app, rather than selling anything – just made sense. I took referral and network marketing, and I updated it for the new paradigm shift. And no matter what brands or products we put on the software, they will be successful, and their customers will be successful. Here is the philosophy I came up with behind the app. I know you will love it:

The Smartr App Philosophy

"The idea of shopping based on "lowest price," helped to catapult us into the recession we are still experiencing today, just as much as any other factors claiming responsibility. Laying off workers, harming the environment, and focusing on shareholders' profits - are bigger problems than most realize. The theory of "lowest price" shopping is based upon consumption, irresponsibility, mass production, and greed, not value - as there is simply no real value in the lowest price.

Before the corporate giants of today emerged, we had mom and pop stores on every corner, healthily competing with their fellow neighbors... in the name of collaboration, not domination. Life was fair. We all knew that value existed in ourselves and our passions, and we didn't have to put other people out of business to put food on our tables. We all knew there was more than enough to go around.

Today, the world is changing rapidly - and time is the real currency. Entrepreneurs are emerging within all of us, simply because we demand freedom now. All we really want, is time - time with our family and friends. We want time to explore the globe, and time to explore ourselves. And we don't want to worry about paying for it either.

So, let me ask you... if we are willing to pay a little extra for first class, "free" refills, or leather interior... If we are willing to pay $20 dollars for headache medicine at the airport, and $5 dollars for a bottle of water to wash it down - simply because of convenience... Would we use a system that disperses profits back to the consumer? Would we be willing to use an app that we can integrate into our everyday lives, that can help reignite the hidden passions in mankind - by providing him with the time, money, and freedom he needs to evolve and thrive? Would we change our habits to bring balance to other people's lives? - Friends and strangers alike? Would we give to others simply because we should?

The Smartr App Company developed our technology on the very same ambition and cooperation that sent us to the moon... you could say, that very same spark that fueled the American dream so long ago. Our "Pass the App" system is not based on greed, lowest price, or domination... and we are definitely not trying to put anyone out of business. We are simply proving to the world that there is a better way to do business. There are better things to do with profits - and easier ways to take care of customers. You know how? By allowing everyone to become successful together... instead of the few people at the top.

Price is only a factor when value is questioned, and the value built in the Smartr App system - is its ability to help bring a little extra income to the average person's pocket. Its ability to allow us to all become successful together. Let's share The Smartr App with our loved ones, and earn enough to start fueling a few dreams... Let's help one another rebuild value in ourselves - by simply, passing the app.

Today.

Today, I am thankful... for each and every day. I will be better every day. I will do more every day. I will greet each day with laughter, love, and gratitude, and say goodnight with a brief reflection of the day's events before I honor my creator for the gift of today. This day was given to me, and should not be taken for granted. I need to concentrate on living in the now, but I will momentarily reflect on the day's events for the sole purpose of seeing what I can improve upon before the sun rises tomorrow and my eyes close tonight. When given the choice to do nothing and take action, I will forever choose to take action. The person who used to do nothing is gone. If this person reappears, I will become aware, take action against them, forgive myself, and move on. TODAY, I TAKE ACTION.

Today, I will become wiser. I will choose to absorb knowledge and educate myself in every subject matter possible, as my thirst for wisdom is a primary driver in my success and freedom. I will condition my body and eternal spirit to make peace with the only enemy I thought I had... my mind. I have spent far too long fighting what I thought was a never ending battle, but not anymore. It is impossible to defeat an enemy that only exists within me. I have no enemies... I have no failures... only opportunities for growth and expansion. TODAY, I GROW. TODAY, I EXPAND. TODAY, I AM WISER.

Today, I will win. Tomorrow I will win. For the rest of my life, I will win. I will be successful. I will be great. My rewards and wealth are a byproduct of the value and service I offer those around me, including myself. The lives I change are my true reward... My success is a byproduct of the lives I change, as well as my decision to change myself. My life is my reward. TODAY, I AM SUCCESSFUL. TODAY, I AM GREAT. TODAY, I WIN.

Today, I overcome. I shall suffer no longer. I will not waste my energy on long-term goals. I will break my long-term goals down into simple daily steps, and instead, devote my energy to becoming the person I must become to reach my long-term goals. Yesterday, I was not that person. Today, I am that person. I am stronger than yesterday; mentally, physically, emotionally, and spiritually. I have not only adapted to, but have overcome the thief that robbed me of fulfilling my destiny yesterday... my mind. TODAY, I AM STRONGER. TODAY, I OVERCOME.

Today, there is no enemy. Today, there is no fear. Not anymore. I am the only thing that has ever stopped me, but today, I forgive myself. I forgive everyone I feel has ever done me wrong, simply because, no one has ever done me wrong. At the time they performed actions which I thought were against me, or wrong, I did not understand myself the way I do now. I can show them compassion, pray for their healing, and hope one day we can sit side by side while I share with them how grateful I am for every breath they take. TODAY, I FORGIVE.

Today, I un-focus. Sometimes people will focus their anger towards me, but I will not focus my anger towards them. I am in control of my feelings, my emotions, and my actions. Only I can make the choice to become upset or angry, and I no longer make that choice. I forgive them. I forgive myself. Pain is necessary, but my suffering is optional. Today I make the decision to never suffer again. TODAY, I AM IN CONTROL.

Today, I realize my purpose. My body belongs to me and so does my mind. And now, I am now in control. This magnificent and beautiful vessel was created for one thing and one thing only... my purpose that God has given me. My destiny that I now realize. It is said that the two most important days of our lives are the day we are born, and the day we realize WHY we were born. For me, that day is today. TODAY, I AM MY PURPOSE.

Today, I make the decision to be wealthy. I make the decision to be healthy. I make the decision to be successful. I make the decision to have a smile on my face even when no one else is smiling. I make the decision to provide for those who cannot provide for themselves. I make the decision to stay in control of my mind. I make the decision to forgive even when I am not forgiven. Today is my purpose. Today is my gift. Today, I am in control. TODAY, IS MY GIFT. TODAY, I TAKE RESPONSIBILITY FOR MY LIFE.

Today, God will move mountains for me, because today, I will move mountains for God. TODAY, I AM READY.

Chapter 2
Build Assets

I will talk in just a little bit about the "empire" mindset, but I need to tell you first, your path to financial freedom starts with building assets. As many as you can have. In whatever form they are available to you.

What is an asset? Simply put; it is something or someone that makes money for you... and the more multipliers you can place behind an asset, the better.

What is a multiplier? This can be more clearly defined as the ability to scale, grow, or expand for little to no money. A landscape or painting company would not scale as well as a software or publishing company. Why? Because no matter how much money you could possibly make from mowing lawns or painting houses, you will always need to put people and equipment in place to take care of those homes. If you write a book, or build a piece of software, the task only needs to be completed one time... and you can sell as many copies as you want.

While most people believe insurance, energy, or pharmaceuticals to be the world's largest industries – the winner goes to "information." Nothing in this world has larger multipliers, or greater retention of value – than information.

BarnesandNoble.com is scalable... a Barnes and Noble store – not so much. Writing a book is great! Owning a publishing company, and gaining royalties from all of the book – can we say, "multiplyer?Do you get it now?

So, why are assets so important?

I was about 20 years old when I started selling insurance and securities at a tiered financial firm, which swore it was not multilevel marketing. MLM or not, we were making money off of, not only recruiting people, but the sales from those recruits as well. As much as this period of my life taught me that I did not want to dress up in a suit and tie every day, it DID teach me the power of making money off the efforts of other people. Too bad I walked away from the industry for no freaking reason at all. There is no telling where my life would have gone.

I am not quite sure why I stayed away from network marketing for so long. After I stopped with the life insurance bit, it wouldn't be 7 years or so before I got back into the asset building game. I spoke in Trainer to Trillionaire about the protein MLM I joined near the end of my personal training career – and even spoke of the trash talking I did about network marketing for years prior. What is funny though, through all of the trash talk, I had completely closed my mind off to the possibility of financial evolution. Now I know that my lack of belief in my ability to build assets truly held me back from growth all of those years. I know this because, even though I was a small business owner, I had not yet started working "smartr." I knew nothing about multipliers, investments, marketing, or business... and my life remained a cycle of average, just like all of those around me. I worked a whole lot, with very little pay off, and had no reason to dream big for much of anything.

After leaving the personal training industry, assets just made sense. And since it had already become readily apparent by now that I would be raising Emma on my own as a stay at home father, I needed a way to build assets. Joining the protein MLM would actually be one of the greatest decisions I would make in my business career up until that point. It allowed me to start dreaming again. I created a vision board. I started working towards real big goals and dreams. I felt like I could actually have and do what I wanted – without a job.

The choice to be a stay at home father is more than likely the reasoning behind the birth of The Smartr App; more so than improving MLM. People deserve the time to do whatever they want to do with their lives. The last thing this world needs is another generation of children raised by television sets and day care providers.

Assets can be multiple things. For real estate investors, assets include homes, apartment buildings, skyscrapers, prisons... Stock investors create assets through the NASDAQ or NYSE. Angel investors invest in projects that are just getting off the ground. Publishing companies own intellectual property by way of books, cartoons, likeness rights to characters.

Most people have one asset, if any. And that asset is usually themselves. People work jobs, and if they quit or get fired, they soon learn about their lack of assets when they have to immediately rush out and find a new job.

Sometimes employees break into self-employment, but this is hardly entrepreneurship. A person becomes fed up with their job, and realize they can get a bit more freedom by doing it for themselves at home; or even performing another task... but until they can walk away from it, and create income without being involved, it is not an asset.

A lot of people break into network marketing, and a very small percentage of them succeed because the system is too hard – they were recruited by someone who doesn't understand the business –

they never learn the concepts of asset building or duplication – they decide they don't want to sell eyelash extensions to achieve financial freedom... the list goes on and on. Many of my reasons for the creation of The Smartr App. I still think MLM has its purpose, so do not think I am trash talking it or anything. It is a very powerful industry with some very amazing people. I just think there are easier ways to do things.

No matter what assets you decide to build though, you have a story, and I promise you – a lot of people can learn from it. This is why I believe in books and publications so much. They are simple assets to create, and they always lead to more. Once someone gets a book out of them, they are going to write another and another. Their new found creativity could lead to more businesses and opportunities, as well as an amalgamation of new, varied content; which is a pure expression and reflection of the person who decided to sit down and write a chapter. Or they could write a book and decide to never do it again. Then be that weird entrepreneur who wrote that one book that one time...

Build a few businesses that work, then publish a book or two about how you got there.

Just as soon as I joined the protein network marketing company did I start finding the problems with the industry. I left that company and started consulting with, rather than promoting others; in hopes to find a solution. It dawned on me that not everyone wants to sell makeup. Or sell protein, then try to force their friends and family to sell It too...

I also learned – people enjoyed hearing me speak. My insight and perspective was useful across the whole spectrum of business, not just sales. Once I started combining my new knowledge with my counseling and coaching capabilities, I learned that no matter what anyone's problems really are; business, relationships, what have you... they were problems long before the business or relationship came along. Everything has to do with everything. Most of us are ignorant to the fact that we are the root cause of the problems we continue to face. And this problem can always be found in the place where people never think to look – the very mind they use to think and make decisions from. Mind is the cause of poverty. Mind is the cause of broken relationships and children who do not listen. Mind is the cause of unhappiness and confusion. Mind is the hardest thing to overcome, because we just don't want to admit we are wrong...

On a happier note, I also learned, no matter what anyone does for a living... no matter how happy they may seem, they can always use more money and time to live a life of freedom and love with their friends and family.

I used to find it so weird, that even from a young age, I was always forced into some sort of leadership role. Whether it was the captain, coach, the manager, or a teacher. No matter the position I was placed in, I was always forced to the top of the hierarchy without having asked for it.

It was the same force of nature that allowed me to find solace in connecting with others on a behavioral and spiritual level. For some reason, every single time I would open my mouth, everyone would shut up and listen. I had a push into the speaking industry right before I left the training realm. It was more than likely the catalyst. Couple that with my new found skills in MLM and sales, and I was actually able to make a living speaking and moving some books.

I was about to leave Camp Hero Fitness when I was invited to speak to a group of 60 or so gym participants one Saturday. As soon as I finished telling my 200-pound weight loss story, I received a standing ovation, and was then invited to speak again. Which led to being invited back again, and again. Before I knew it, a couple of months had passed, and I was still training clients at Camp Hero, simply because of the Saturday speaking gig. After hearing, "you need to write a book about your story" from about a dozen people, I decided to do it.

Nine grueling months of writing, editing, transcribing, writing, and editing some more tested me to the core. I was making a living, but it wasn't a good living. I was making just enough to keep faith in my vision; no more, no less. After publishing my first book, some silly part of me thought sales would come flocking. After getting attention from some publishers, I just kept writing books. I fought a custody case. I fought an ex-girlfriend and her minions...

I was so proud after my first book – to tell people I was an author. Just as much as I enjoyed the initials which followed my name after becoming a trainer and a nutritionist. And like I said earlier, it's funny to think about all of the books I have on the market, and have had on the market for some time. Now I write because I concentrate on "being." Writing is part of who I am, and who I am supposed to be. I definitely do not need to introduce myself as an author to define who I am. Books are just as much a spiritual decision for me now as much as they are a business decision.

I thought my world was over when the minions started posting bad reviews on my books... but then I ended up having a news story go viral, and it caused a lot of books to be downloaded. Then, the attention subsided. Why? Because, what the heck was I doing with my life that would condone anyone buying one of my books? And, again, the authors I have helped with my publishing company who are upset when their books do not sell any copies either.

Creating businesses is who I am. Creating content is who I am. To save and change the world is who I am. And who I am, is who you are. We are all writers, and content creators, and speakers. We all have a story in us that someone would love to hear – if we are willing to share it. I don't want to be known for being a content creator. I would rather be known for being the guy who saved the entire planet, he just happened to make great freaking content at the same time.

Today.

Today, I am thankful... for each and every day. I will be better every day. I will do more every day. I will greet each day with laughter, love, and gratitude, and say goodnight with a brief reflection of the day's events before I honor my creator for the gift of today. This day was given to me, and should not be taken for granted. I need to concentrate on living in the now, but I will momentarily reflect on the day's events for the sole purpose of seeing what I can improve upon before the sun rises tomorrow and my eyes close tonight. When given the choice to do nothing and take action, I will forever choose to take action. The person who used to do nothing is gone. If this person reappears, I will become aware, take action against them, forgive myself, and move on. TODAY, I TAKE ACTION.

Today, I will become wiser. I will choose to absorb knowledge and educate myself in every subject matter possible, as my thirst for wisdom is a primary driver in my success and freedom. I will condition my body and eternal spirit to make peace with the only enemy I thought I had... my mind. I have spent far too long fighting what I thought was a never ending battle, but not anymore. It is impossible to defeat an enemy that only exists within me. I have no enemies... I have no failures... only opportunities for growth and expansion. TODAY, I GROW. TODAY, I EXPAND. TODAY, I AM WISER.

Today, I will win. Tomorrow I will win. For the rest of my life, I will win. I will be successful. I will be great. My rewards and wealth are a byproduct of the value and service I offer those around me, including myself. The lives I change are my true reward... My success is a byproduct of the lives I change, as well as my decision to change myself. My life is my reward. TODAY, I AM SUCCESSFUL. TODAY, I AM GREAT. TODAY, I WIN.

Today, I overcome. I shall suffer no longer. I will not waste my energy on long-term goals. I will break my long-term goals down into simple daily steps, and instead, devote my energy to becoming the person I must become to reach my long-term goals. Yesterday, I was not that person. Today, I am that person. I am stronger than yesterday; mentally, physically, emotionally, and spiritually. I have not only adapted to, but have overcome the thief that robbed me of fulfilling my destiny yesterday... my mind. TODAY, I AM STRONGER. TODAY, I OVERCOME.

Today, there is no enemy. Today, there is no fear. Not anymore. I am the only thing that has ever stopped me, but today, I forgive myself. I forgive everyone I feel has ever done me wrong, simply because, no one has ever done me wrong. At the time they performed actions which I thought were against me, or wrong, I did not understand myself the way I do now. I can show them compassion, pray for their healing, and hope one day we can sit side by side while I share with them how grateful I am for every breath they take. TODAY, I FORGIVE.

Today, I un-focus. Sometimes people will focus their anger towards me, but I will not focus my anger towards them. I am in control of my feelings, my emotions, and my actions. Only I can make the choice to become upset or angry, and I no longer make that choice. I forgive them. I forgive myself. Pain is necessary, but my suffering is optional. Today I make the decision to never suffer again. TODAY, I AM IN CONTROL.

Today, I realize my purpose. My body belongs to me and so does my mind. And now, I am now in control. This magnificent and beautiful vessel was created for one thing and one thing only... my purpose that God has given me. My destiny that I now realize. It is said that the two most important days of our lives are the day we are born, and the day we realize WHY we were born. For me, that day is today. TODAY, I AM MY PURPOSE.

Today, I make the decision to be wealthy. I make the decision to be healthy. I make the decision to be successful. I make the decision to have a smile on my face even when no one else is smiling. I make the decision to provide for those who cannot provide for themselves. I make the decision to stay in control of my mind. I make the decision to forgive even when I am not forgiven. Today is my purpose. Today is my gift. Today, I am in control. TODAY, IS MY GIFT. TODAY, I TAKE RESPONSIBILITY FOR MY LIFE.

Today, God will move mountains for me, because today, I will move mountains for God. TODAY, I AM READY.

Chapter 3
Solace in the process...

I have been working on a rather large business book for quite some time. It has even changed names a few times, depending on where I was in my journey at the time. I promise I will publish it someday, but for now, I have added a bit of content here. The book's first title was, "The Automated Marketking," before it changed to, "The Enlightened Entrepreneurs' Guide to Kicking Ass." The subtitle was long enough to take up the front cover lol. We will see what I name it... but for now, here is some good content we can all learn from:

The sad thing about these movies and shows that show how a billion-dollar business is born, is there is not enough time in the day to possible grasp the struggle an entrepreneur will go through. And I can promise you, the way we have been taught to do business in the past no longer holds any weight this day and age.

Most businesses start undercapitalized, and rarely get off the ground because people are afraid of bootstrapping. The Social Network makes it seem like those guys were living in close quarters and eating a shitty diet for weeks; not months, or years. No one knows Mark Cuban's Story, or Colonial Sanders story. Whenever Hollywood does spit out another Steve Jobs movie at us – they will never be able to capture the essence of starving, living in your car, worrying about feeding your child – night, after night, after night. And this struggle, can last for years, if you are willing. Most just aren't. 97% of the population are employees, who work for the 3% of entrepreneurs.

If an employee does make the switch over to entrepreneurship – all they really have to follow are bad examples – led by an entire industry of entrepreneurs who have figured out how to strip money away from the newly self-employed who have been feed bad information. Entire insurance, benefits, investment and law firms, among many other BS scam artists are more than willing to tell or teach you how to be an entrepreneur. In reality, all you really have to endure is a test from God.

I say that we need to find solace in the process of following through on an idea, because the process is not going away. It may seem like you have found a shortcut or two during the process, but the shortcut, and even the perception of the shortcut – is still part of the process. Most people want to achieve something major in their life, but they forget about the small things it will take to get there. You want to own a publishing company? Write a dozen books first… but remember that even publishing one book, starts with sitting down to write a chapter. You want to find your soulmate? Maybe you need to start with feeling better about yourself today. You want to launch an app? Sometimes, you have to wait for app testers and their slower-than-average review process… only after months and months of tests, errors, and headaches.

Having a vision or a goal gives you a finish line… and that means you are millions of steps ahead of most people on the planet. If you already know where you are going to end up, then obviously, whatever you are dealing with now is part of the process. Just don't give up. Don't quit. Always know that whatever you want, wants you… and it is right around the corner, waiting for you to get there. Most people don't have a goal. Most people don't have a finish line… Some people don't even have legs. You will make it. I promise you.

Now, take a gander at a little eBook I wrote called:

Understanding Manifestation

I like to blog and write about ideas. While learning to market myself, I started taking those little ideas and turning them into ninety-nine cent eBooks. It allowed me to get my name out there and make some extra change while I was building my businesses. A year of writing later, I am almost sickened by the first books I published. While people still give me accolades on those early manuscripts... I see amateur writing, but I do see promise. Through speaking and writing more, I have fine-tuned my message a bit and I do not stammer nearly as often as I used to. Editing publications seems to go a lot faster now because I make fewer mistakes when freewriting. I have also experienced insurmountable spiritual growth and insight in the last 400 days or so too. And you may be reading this on a comic book sized paperback because I decided to no longer publish any manuscripts by eBook only. I want readers to be able to physically hold my writing from now on.

Those who know me also know I like to repeat myself. I do things like, add an eBook into a new book that I am writing, or a paste in a section for reference from another book. I call these, affirmations. I believe I touch on more affirmations in *Understanding the God Theory*, but obviously, *Understanding Manifestation Second Edition* focuses on manifestation. I do not necessarily believe we learn more about a book by reading by reading it a second time, just like I do not believe we simply progress by saying affirmations over and over. I believe we learn more about ourselves. I believe affirmations allow us to see how far we are willing to go, based on something as questionable as faith.

All too often we are in a different state of mind when experiencing life, be it, a movie, book, or song. I show my daughter some of the cartoons I watched when I was a little kid and immediately turn them off. I did not realize then just how sarcastic some of those loons were when I was her age. Being who I am now, I realize a lot of those cartoons turned me into the person I am today. A person that I have worked diligently to change these last few great years. Like many in my generation, I grew up being brainwashed by relentless television watching, so I make sure to limit Emma's exposure to it; along with her tablet, and cell phones. As of right now, she is not allowed on the computer. Most of her free time, we are playing together, or she is drawing, coloring, building or creating something. I want to keep her imagination active as long as possible, as I know I have spent years trying to replace movie quotes and song lyrics embedded in my subconscious since birth.

Regardless of the thoughts we have in our mind, The Law of Assumption teaches us that reality is subjective, and it changes based on a person's perspective of their life and their knowledge of the universe. The Law of Attraction brings us into alignment with whatever we are thinking about. Manifestation is the process by which all of this magic takes place.

Hold onto Your Vision. No Matter What.

In both Trainer to Trillionaire and Outgrow, there was a section about success and happiness. About happiness being a choice rather than circumstantial. A temporary state of being rather than an ultimate goal.

We have three minds: Our conscious mind, our subconscious mind, and our spiritual mind. The conscious mind is the constant chatter. Our ideas and our identity. The noise that goes on regardless if you are listening or not. Most of it is useless ideas, the movie quotes I mentioned earlier, and fears other people placed in there for us. This part of our mind is filled with the paradigms which were taught to us before we had the ability to make conscious decisions of our own. I am constantly asking myself if a particular thought actually belongs to me or someone else. Dozens of times per day I reflect on old thoughts and decide whether or not I should being working to get rid of them. Remember, your life will never be any better than the language you are using. Language can be words, art, expression, thoughts, dreams...

The subconscious mind is the body. A master computer grabbing thoughts from the chatter of the conscious mind, and turning these thoughts into new habits and ideals. Anytime one of these thoughts is acted upon a foreign number of times, the body will begin to accept this as a habit by forming an addiction to the action. This is done through our hormone receptors by releasing dopamine at the sense of satisfaction once the newly formed habit is accomplished. If we follow through on the new addiction even further, our body will become reliant upon the addiction. And we are never truly satisfied, since addiction means you are repeatedly trying to fill a void which can never be filled by an action you no longer wish to perform. This cycle keeps us going. I know this book is not about addictions, but I wanted you to have a better understanding of what the subconscious mind really does. Any information embedded in the subconscious long enough will become a part of our reality.

Before the age of 7, we are nothing but a subconscious mind. A physical and emotional being of creation. Ready to take on the world with little to no limitations. Recording and absorbing all of the information we are surrounded with, while learning and watching our parent's habits. Learning how to stress about work and relationships. Learning how to become an employee. Learning how to become a dull, lifeless person without a vision. Even a characteristic as simple as tapping your foot while sitting still is more than likely a habit you developed from your parents or peers.

Once we hit the age of 7, our cognitive mind kicks in. We can now discern between cause and effect. We realize there is now reverberating resonance in the frequency we are creating and we choose not to create. Of course, I am certain most children do not know of those words, but you get the picture.

Think about times you reacted to a situation. Perhaps, someone said something to you, or performed an action against you. Your reaction caused your emotional state to change. You immediately became happy, or sad, though completely unaware why the shift in consciousness took place. This is more than likely because you do not contain a memory to associate with your emotional state. The habit was engrained so deep into your subconscious mind before becoming aware of the thinking mind, that your body and your emotions took over, at which point, you are usually left looking like a fool and explaining your deepest apologies to someone.

Most of us are unaware of, not only the intentions we are placing upon the field of energy we all live in, but also, our ability to change this field based on which state of being we are walking in at that very moment. The energy we produce with our bodies changes the energy of all of our surroundings. The people we are around. Our pets, plants... this book. I was even watching a documentary where this neurologist stuck diodes in a cup of yogurt across the room from a gentleman making phone calls to people that typically caused him stress, and the probiotics and live bacteria in the yogurt were reacting in real time to the emotional state of unrest coming from this man. Imagine how many objects in your immediate surroundings at this very moment are embodied with your stress patterns. Kind of makes you want to apologize to your bottle of water, huh? Perhaps even tell her you love her before you enjoy the life which it brings into your body.

We must become aware that we are not our parents. We are not our genetics or our habits. We are not the answers society gave us before we were even aware of our minds. We are the observer of our choices. We are the awareness of the decisions we have made. If you put this book down, and take a moment to think about your life; I want you to take pride in becoming whole heartedly aware that this life... your life is a mere byproduct of your choices. Your thoughts and decisions. Nothing more. Take responsibility, live contently from this moment forward, and if you want a different outcome, make different choices.

We can always change the outcome. And the best part is, we don't even need to know how. We just need to know what we want. We must create a vision for ourselves. This brings in the universal laws which guide our entire universe of being. They have always been working for you whether you were aware or not... Giving you exactly what you were feeling and thinking about.

Breaking our subconscious habits takes nothing more than making different choices. Disciplining ourselves to follow through on our vision so we can indeed create this new way of life we wish to live. This repetitive practice of forming new habits becomes easier and easier, as it is no different than training new muscles at the gym. At first, there may be a little soreness. Some nodding off, or some fatigue. But if you follow through, the payoff will be exponential. This quantum field of energy which binds us all will start working in your favor. As a matter of fact, it has always been working in your favor. You were just unaware of your ability to change it. There has never been anything wrong in your life, ever. Your conscious awareness has been waiting for your discovery of your "self" and your power.

Why not actively start creating your new life rather than reacting and running your life in a self-contained survival mode? Why wait for a crisis to strike that will force you into change, rather than holding onto a desire for change? Crises happen simply because of making multiple decisions over and over again which do not align with your purpose. The decisions of the subconscious habits, created from the conscious paradigms and ideas of other people cause the likely outcomes of our lives. Once we take a thought from the conscious mind, and embed it in the subconscious mind, a new habit is formed; a new seed is planted and ready for growth. New cells are born. Billions of old cells with emotional ideals and habits die as your new cells with the new idea of the "you" that you wish to be is formed.

When I think of chronic diseases... I think of people being stuck in their old thought processes. As nearly all illness is caused by our own thought process and emotional state, rather than outside forces, we decide to remain sick or in ill health. We decide to carry around our (dis)ease out of habit and lack of desire to grow. If we can carry with us a new vision of being healed, eventually our old idea of sickness will die too. This will make way for the new you; a healed you.

I remember back around the end of 2012... I was still working in the corporate gym environment, and getting ready to make my departure to become a self-employed trainer. The only thing was, I became a trainer to help people, not to cash in. Not to make oodles of money, (as personal training definitely will not make someone extremely rich... and yes, I said oodles) but to help others achieve the happiness and fulfillment I had created in my own body and mind. Becoming my subconscious mind again, rather than being stuck in the wave of influence of the paradigms that had been holding me back until then. Becoming a trainer was the beginning process in my remembrance of who I used to be.

One day, without thinking, I spoke the starting point of my vision into existence. I said to myself, "By the end of 2013, I will be able to train anyone I want to, for free."

I had no idea how. I just knew what I wanted, and I began to tell everyone. I told every friend and every family member. Every client. People would even ask me how I was going to make this possible or pay my bills, to which I usually responded, "I don't know."

As silly as it sounded, it was my vision. My dream. The frontal lobe, which plays a key role in envisioning the life we desire, became alive. I held onto my vision (my idea) and chose not to give up on my belief, regardless of what anyone else told me. Negative feedback became welcomed simply because negative feedback is sometimes necessary to set you back on course with what it is you are really going after. The point is, you have to hold the vision and not give up. Who cares about how you are going to get there?

By 2013, I was introduced to network marketing and motivational speaking. Because of both of these, I was able to start training my clients for absolutely free. Not only was I able to replace my income, I was able to start dreaming in a big way, and constantly looking for ways to bring in more passive income so I could do the things I wanted to do. I was finally able to start enjoying life. And it happened so fast, it took me by complete surprise. Of course, my vision has also changed significantly since then, and now I follow through on just about any and every idea that could possibly come into my mind. Never underestimate the power of a journal, a sticky note, or a tape recorder. Your dreams should be updated as often as you can.

You are the creator of your world. Nature is completely neutral and the universe is waiting for you to take action and work aggressively towards building your legacy. Whatever it is you want or desire is already manifested for you in the spiritual world; the universal stream of abundance. Your subjective consciousness will create the end result for you as soon as you become the person it will take to manifest that reality. This rarely has as much to do with 'doing' as it does acting, becoming, and envisioning.

No matter how expensive a microscope you can purchase, you will never find an oak tree inside an acorn. Though, the acorn uses the law of attraction to fulfill its purpose, just as we should. The same energy the acorn uses for growth, is composed of the same elements which inhabit your inner most desire for growth and success. What is the difference between you and the acorn? The acorn believes. The acorn will never question its destiny. The acorn trusts in God and nature, and becomes the oak tree, regardless of anyone's opinions of how small the acorn is. You will hear negative opinions or gain undesired feedback, or just stop caring, and your dream has the ability to diminish if you allow it.

People hear of the law of attraction and still have entitlements and expect handouts. The word attraction has "action" imbedded in the word. In your life, you are going to be confronted with opportunities to act, and some of those will be scary as shit. The opportunities that take you out of your comfort zone are usually the best ones to act upon. You need to take action to become whoever it is you have to be to receive your abundance, now.

Think of a farmer standing in front of a freshly plowed field. In one hand, he holds a seed of corn. In the other, a seed for nightshade, a deadly poison. If he plants both seeds in the ground, waters and nurtures the seeds, by the end of the season he will have both a corn stalk, and a stalk of poison. The field did not care what he planted... only that he planted and nurtured the seeds. The universe returned both in exchange.

You can order a pair of shoes from a shop online. You tell them you need a size 10. They process your order and send out the shoes without a care in the world as to whether or not they fit or if you will like them. They do not know you, or if you will actually find the shoes to be comfortable. You asked, and you received. The process was followed through to completion regardless of your feelings about the process.

Some of the following has come from a couple of my books, even though I have edited and added to the entirety of Understanding Manifestation. Though, repetitive action is the key to success. When we have a chance to hear, watch, or read something that will change our life for the better, we should bring it into a consistent state of practice. One of my internet mentors, Bob Proctor, still carries his first copy of Think and Grow Rich, and he reads this book on a daily basis, even after decades of having read it before. At the end of this chapter, I will share one of my favorite success stories with you, so stay tuned.

We need to take advantage of every opportunity. After all, we are creating them with our choices.

– Jason Criddle

Happiness is not a long-term goal. It is a choice... no different than any other choice you can make. And that very choice is going to be a major key in building relationships with other people as well as yourself. It is so refreshing to meet a total stranger who is taking time out of their day to be overly friendly to fellow strangers. While some may think this is a cry out for attention, I feel this person is free. Aware of their own free will, true self, and purpose. If you have to convince yourself you are happy... keep working at it. Your happiness is only as strong as your belief in yourself. It must be unwavering, no matter how unstable the foundation around you may seem to be getting. Love is the gateway and truth to happiness. He who does not hear the music, think the dancer is crazy.

Success too, will never have a stopping point. After redirecting my focus, and changing the people I associated with throughout the many courses my life took, I began analyzing some of the major behavioral characteristics of some of the wealthiest and most successful people I surrounded myself with. Not as to compare them to others... just to see what set them apart. All those with whom I engaged were interested in others and interesting themselves; curious, inclusive, attentive, open about their struggles, open-minded, and humble. It struck me that those are not generally qualities or characteristics we apply to 'masters' and mystics of the universe. Quite the contrary, we more often use words such as self-centered or egocentric. Maybe even boring, dull, self-centered, or bland. Even when I was nearly 400 pounds, I used to think of fit or in-shape people to the same degree. After becoming fit myself, I realized reality was quite different – the exact opposite in most cases. I was the self-centered egocentric, as I spent all of my time thinking of myself. Always trying to gain as much as I could while harnessing anger and not giving the greatest parts of myself to others.

We should always look for opportunities to reconsider our perception about others... especially when questioning or analyzing effective roles of leadership and how these leaders may conduct themselves in their businesses or life in general. Sometimes we must find the best traits in others, and the worst traits of our own, in order to learn from them.

So, what makes a person successful? I do not believe there is a definitive list. If there were a list, it would always be added to, by numerous people from all over the globe. One trait that sets a winner apart from the rest of the world, they look for and find opportunities where others see nothing. As humans, we will always find what we are looking for. If we are looking for positive data to support a claim, or negative feedback to give us reason to give up, it will appear. If we are craving an immediate desire for success, our environment will shift in order to deliver the success we are craving. You must still work on your 'self' for this shift to take place.

You must find a lesson where others will only see a problem. You realize by now, any and everything that happens to us, can be an opportunity to learn. Stay focused on creating solutions and results, rather than solving problems. This way, you will only encounter solutions and results. It may be difficult to realize this, especially during hardships, but there has absolutely never been anything wrong in your life, ever. Think of problems as welcomed circumstances which will manifest growth. Deal with your problems and challenges quickly and effectively to gain wisdom from the situation. Don't just put your head in the sand. I will say again, face your challenges and use them as opportunities to grow and learn more about yourself. You can tell the size of a person's will by the size of the problem that bothers them. What kind of person do you want to be?

Keep a mental log of what works and what doesn't, that way, you waste zero time on what no longer serves you. For example, if you have a flawless sales script, and it takes you three minutes to get to the point to where you keep losing stability, and therefore losing your prospect – become completely efficient at the first 3 minutes. Then practice it so much, it becomes muscle memory – an afterthought. Now you can focus all of your effort on driving past that portion that was holding you back. I promise you, if you are learning to ride and bicycle and you keep staring at a tree, you will steer directly towards the tree. You have to completely drown out the tree. Get rid of the obstacle in your mind before beginning. Visualize the path, and stay productive on the path. Practice makes permanent.

You must surround yourself with like-minded people. Discover the importance of synergy and start creating win-win relationships. There are many a benefit from being part of a bigger team. No matter how many ideas one person can come up with, more people can come up with more ideas. More perspectives can find more innovative solutions to existing ideas. You are the average of the five people you spend the most time with. Be sure to surround yourself with people who share your vision and have your ultimate goals in mind as well. Even if they are not walking the same path with you, they should at least be a part of your award-winning support team. Be sure to support their vision and path as well.

That said, take this advice to heart about people you feel the need to associate with... DO NOT SURROUND YOURSELF WITH TOXIC PEOPLE. Average people are attracted to and comfortable associating with other average people. Do you wish to remain average? If you have people in your life holding you back from what you want, you must make a change.

Remember, you and only you create your success. You must become consciously and methodically aware of your vision, and work to manifest the reality you desire. Others seem to hope success will find them. You seek, so you shall find. Success will find you if you are the person, with the path, ready to receive the success. You must become the source of what you seek. If you are wanting something more, what are you willing to give to receive it?

You must overcome and embrace fear. We are taught throughout our lives to be fearless. Fear is not only necessary; it also makes us stronger. Fight or flight mode is created by the feelings and emotions we place upon a situation, and that rush of hormones typically comes from the unfamiliar, or replaying past experiences. That situation you are afraid of is usually one which will allow is to grow into a greater person. This is why we feel the initial bout of fear to begin with. This is your body being faced with what used to be a limitation, and your mind being given the decision to finally overcome it. All too often, we look for ways to go around what we are afraid of, but then we never become better. A successful person is just as fearful as everyone else; however, they are not controlled or limited by their fears. They look for opportunities to break these barriers down and kick fear in the ass.

Don't always think you have the answers when you should be focused more so on asking the right questions. You must limit yourself from certain thoughts and situations to allow room for the right thoughts and situations. Only ask questions which will place you in a productive, creative, and positive state of emotions. Stop thinking you know it all, as knowing rids us the ability to ever truly know.

Do not complain about your life or place blame on others. This will only place you in a negative state of mind. Not only is it a waste of time and emotions, it is a waste of valuable energy. (inner-chi) A negative state of mind is an unproductive state to be in. Stress causes cortisol to be released into the bloodstream which cuts off our ability to problem solve and think critically. This time you are spending not taking responsibility for your actions and outcomes, or lack thereof. This is time you could be creating, planning, and/or serving other people. When you feel someone isn't treating you the way you should be treated, this is a simple misunderstanding and should clearly show you that more time is needed to become the person you need to become to have the life you desire. You are in complete control of your emotional state. Blaming someone for your negativity will not solve anything.

Make up what you lack in talent with skill. And practice that skill, with a ridiculous work ethic. As I said earlier, practice makes permanent. Most successful people find proficient ways to maximize the potential in their 'self' in every way they can. The key to simplification, is duplication. Find what works for you by achieving the maximum amount of results with as little effort as possible. This will take practice. Be willing to outwork and outsmart everyone. Use every available resource you have more effectively. Realize you are the only person that has ever held you back from attaining what you want.

There is a huge difference between being productive or proactive, and being busy. A job keeps you busy. Just about anything can keep you busy actually. If you want to keep a man from thinking about his future, give him a job where his salary depends on him never thinking about his future. Even sitting in silence, thinking, reading, or watching television can be proactive if you are actually learning and applying what you are learning. If you ever find yourself with nothing to do... never mind. You should never find yourself with nothing to do, even if sitting still and grounding yourself in the now is what needs to be done.

Becoming successful takes living and having fun. Not merely surviving. You must have ambition to ride the ride of a sheer amazing life. Why live your life on autopilot when you can take control? You must create clarity and certainty about what you want (and don't want) in your life. Take time to visualize and plan out your reality so that your reality is not part of someone else's. Create the ending to your story and start taking active steps to direct your life towards that goal. This is as simple as envisioning the wish fulfilled and living in the assumption and feeling that it has already manifested itself. Most people are simply spectators of their own lives. Do you want to be a spectator of yours?

Always innovate. Never imitate. If you are going to take the time to make something better, make it so. Even now, I inserted this eBook into this story, but throughout my editing, I am realizing how much my writing has matured. I am less than halfway through with the editing portion of Understanding Manifestation and I have already added well over a thousand words. I created these short stories for this very reason, but why not add in a little innovation and a lot more value for you, the reader? Giving anything half of the effort will give you half of the desired results in return. You are completely unique to this world and this universe; to God and creation as we know it. You and only you have your gift, and you and only you can share your gift with the world. Just remember the world is waiting.

> *"Either write something worth doing, or do something worth writing."*
>
> **– Benjamin Franklin**

Successful people refuse to procrastinate and don't spend their life waiting for the "right time." I find far too many people waiting for their big break or motivation. What is a big break? What is motivation? I have heard far too many times the answer to someone's financial woes are either winning the lottery, or they are waiting for something big to happen to them. The problem with this is, no one ever has any valid points to support their argument of what "something big," really is. If you are waiting for the perfect time or the right time to make something happen, you will take your ideas to your grave. I believe in fate, destiny, chance, luck, etc., however, I will not wait for any of these ideals to determine or shape my future. I believe in, and I am committed to actively and consciously creating my very own best life.

It took my 9 months to write Trainer to Trillionaire, a 24,000-word book. Unleashing Mind Power will have well over 100,000 words when completed, and it took me less than a month to write it. I used to wait for a muse, or motivation, or some kind of external force to guide me or put me in the mood to create… now it just flows. All I do is make the decision to sit and write, or go out and talk, or make a sale. Whatever it is, I believe our motivation comes from our decisions.

Become a life-long learner. Become a master student. You owe it to yourself and the world to never stop learning about experiences that will help guide you through life, and let go of experiences and thoughts that have held you back up until now. You must constantly work at educating yourself, either formally (academically), informally (watching, listening, asking, reading, student of life) or experientially (doing, trying) … or all three. I am constantly asked where I attended college or where I obtained my degree; most people find it hard to believe I nearly dropped out of high school and I educated myself in what I teach. I worked on my "self" as much as possible and became the person I needed to become to achieve my goals. Whenever I wanted to educate someone in a subject, I learned, learned, and learned some more so I could explain it simply. I wanted to be able to help others conceptualize the message that I needed them to grasp to help guide them towards their future. It wasn't until later that I realized my body was merely a vessel for the God within me.

Remain an optimist. While some may call this the glass half full mentality, I prefer to think of it as, at least there is something in the glass. Truth be told, if I were hard at work and two people were sitting around arguing about the glass being half full or empty, I would drink their water and get back to work. A positive or negative outlook is based upon the opinions of people, it has absolutely nothing to do with reality. In reality, there is only a glass of water awaiting consumption.

If you only grind on the days you feel like grinding, you won't get much done. Consistently do what you need to do, irrespective of how you may feel on a given day. If you are tired of starting over, stop quitting. Successful people rarely live life by stopping and starting. They live life, going and rarely stop taking steps to achieve their desired results.

Take calculated risks... not unnecessary risks. Risks are an important part of growth. Financial, emotional, professional, and psychological risks will take you places you never dreamed of going. Step outside of your box. Do things others would never be willing to do. Don't get yourself hurt and do not hurt others in the process, but take a leap of faith as often as you can.

Many people are reactive. Stay proactive and respond rather than reacting. Think like a chess player and always stay a few moves ahead. Think about the amount of opportunities that will cease to "happen" to you if you are only focused on making things happen to others. Think about the amount of energy you can direct towards your future goals rather than fixing past mistakes. Take action before action is necessary. Hope for the best, and expect the best. Envision the best, and the best will happen.

Do not be a slave to your emotions. Just like fears, successful people feel emotions too. However, they have gained what I like to call, emotional intelligence, and emotional resilience. They stay in a state of being which will only serve the good of themselves and others while always remaining aware of how their emotional state and actions can affect those around them. An emotionally resilient and intelligent leader would never intentionally perform an action that would make another person lose control, just as they would never allow themselves to lose control either.

Become an effective communicator. Take active steps towards becoming a more effective speaker. There are classes, networking groups, books, seminars, dvds… virtually endless amounts of correspondence available for you to learn from so you can get your message across to your audience. Regardless of what message you wish to get across, you must be understood and you must be passionate about your message or others will not be passionate about you. You must amaze people. You must be able to give them a reason to listen to you, believe in you, and want to be a part of your vision.

The act of planning is necessary, but not in the ways most people think. I do not believe a well thought out plan is something that is put on paper to reference every step of the way. I believe a well thought out plan requires a brief moment of brainstorming followed by drastic action to change the "self." You will need to have a plan for your life and work methodically at turning that plan into a reality so your life is no longer a series of unplanned events and outcomes.

I mentioned this earlier, but your desire to be exceptional means that you are typically to do things that most others will not do. You become exceptional by choice, no by consequence. Successful people, who are busy doing, will rarely take time out of their day to talk to you about the things you are not doing. Success will lie forever dormant, until you "do." Doing will lie forever dormant, while you are talking and not acting. There are no coincidences on this plain of existence, only opportunities that can set your life on a completely different course, and the thoughts and fears that can kill those opportunities. We are all faced with live-shaping decisions, every moment of every day. Successful people make the decisions that most will not, cannot, and do not.

Many people are pleasure junkies and not only lack self-control, they also avoid pain and discomfort at all costs. Leaders and success seekers understand the value and benefit of working through the tough times that most people enjoy avoiding. Any opportunity to learn is a good opportunity. An opportunity to teach is a better one. Always take advantage of those moments when you can practice self-control. Understand the importance of discipline in your actions and be happy to take the road less travelled. Stop making decisions that will only gratify the immediate moment and start doing things that will change and shape your life.

Identify your core morals and values and do your best to live your life in accordance with those values. Do not push these values on other people. You don't even have to make them aware of your values or let it be known you will not deviate from your beliefs without proper knowledge or consideration. If you are living in your truth, people will follow your example and never question you.

Introduce yourself to the idea of balance. People who are only successful on a financial level are not successful at all. People who are only happy in a relationship are not really happy at all, simply because there is no balance. Money and success are not interchangeable. We live in a society that teaches us that money equals success. Like many other things, money is just a tool. It's certainly not a bad thing but ultimately, it's just another resource to gain access to what it is you really want. Too many people worship money while their focus should be on having a reason or meaning behind wanting money. Balance in wealth comes when you have created an environment of stability, happiness, and value you can share with others. Everything you touch turns to gold because of what you can do for others, not yourself. Money has no inherit value of any sort. Money is completely worthless. It is the person using the money who holds the value.

Remain humble and stay secure in your skin. Be confident in your abilities, but not arrogant. Your sense of worth is not derived from what you own, who you know, where you live, or what look like. Your sense of worth comes from how you make others feel. Your sense of worth comes from the value you add to other's lives. Never, for a moment believe you are better than anyone or anything else. Remain generous and kind. Always take pleasure in uplifting others and making them look and feel good as well as helping them too achieve their goals and dreams. Be happy to admit to mistakes and apologize when needed. You are equal to every man, woman, and child alive. You are God's equal as well.

Be adaptable and embrace change. Nature forces us to find a balance of comfort and habit. Become comfortable with the new and the unfamiliar. The only way your habits will change is if you are ready to change. You cannot think your way into acting, you must act your way into thinking.

To be successful you will want to keep yourself in shape physically as well. I know that I used to be a trainer and a competitive athlete, so this is not to be mistaken with training for the Olympics or being obsessed with your body unless it serves you. You want to have a basic understanding of nutrition and understand the importance of being physically well. Your body is not who you are, but it is where you live. If you do not have time to learn about the body, at least hire someone to help you learn.

You will want to have a bigger and stronger engine than everyone. Laziness should not be a word in your vocabulary. Outlast everyone. Become completely resilient to the ideas of failure or giving up. Most people warm up, if anything. So few would prefer to throw in the towel when times get hard. You are just warming up when times get hard. Practice using your off switch. Know when to have fun and relax... remember what you have, what you are doing, why you are doing it, and have a blast doing it too. Your passion will only feel like work if you are doing it right, but do not confuse the word "work" for overuse of effort. Anything that will cause negativity or stress will send you in the wrong direction of the stream of abundance. Whenever you feel overworked, ground yourself in the now.

Embrace haters. Embrace negative feedback. Embrace people who are not doing anything with their lives. Embrace constructive criticism. Embrace people who do not want you to succeed. The people who do not like us will offer a different perspective than those who love and follow us. Listen to and act upon feedback. These tests are here for you to become better. In some cases, these people are in this world for no other reason than to stop you from achieving your goal. Stop investing time or emotional energy into people and things you have no control over. Instead, become aware of and act accordingly. Practice compassion and forgiveness.

Become comfortable spending time alone. Do not respond to everything or everyone. You don't have to respond to every email or text message right away. Your time is important. Spend a good amount of your day in solitude either thinking or practicing mediation. Make prayer and manifestation a practice as well. Most men's problems stem from his inability to sit alone in a quiet room. We are all multi-dimensional, amazing, and wonderfully complex creatures - not only physical and psychological beings, but emotional and spiritual creatures as well. Consciously work at being healthy and productive on all levels, even when lost in thought. Your spirituality is the driving force behind anything you wish to accomplish, so make time for God.

Set higher standards for yourself, and if others do not meet those standards, distance yourself from them immediately. Higher standards produce a greater commitment, more momentum, a better work ethic, and of course, better results. You are worth it.

Look for ways to succeed and do not try to rationalize failure. While many are talking about their age, their sore back, their lack of time or opportunities, their poor genetics, or their "bad luck," you will be finding ways to succeed despite any challenges. You will see common setbacks as strengths. You will get off your ass regardless of what people think about themselves or about you, because you are what matters.

Lastly, successful people practice what they preach. Their career is not their identity; it's just their job. It's not who they are, it's just what they do. They are more interested in taking on tasks effectively more so than taking the easy way out. They don't talk about theory; instead, they live in reality; in constant search of whatever course of action will produce desired results over the long term. This will allow you to finish what you start. While so many of us spend our lives starting things that we never finish, successful people get the job done even after the novelty has worn off.

Keep Holding On. Don't Give Up. Ever.

If we can hold onto our vision, regardless of what is going on around us, we will stay in the mode of creation. If we refuse to respond to circumstances in our outside environment, we become even more powerful. This is not to say, we cannot get upset. There is always room for embracing negative emotion. But don't hold onto it. Let it have its time, and let it pass through you. Holding the vision creates oneness. A unity between us and our creator. Our higher self. Having negative thoughts or emotions sends an unbalanced signal to the universe and hinders our desires to manifest.

The brain is a highly adaptive piece of equipment in which changes constant. Neuroplasticity occurs when there are changes in neural pathways and synapses. This is due to changes in behavior, environment, neural processes, thinking, emotions, goals, desires, as well as changes resulting from bodily injury or stress. A habit can be seen as a super-highway of information, where our firing neurons are driving cars. A new idea is a new exit, leading to a new road for the cars to drive on. The proactive approach of creating a new habit then turns the exit into a new freeway, until the old idea becomes an old rickety bridge that the cars no longer drive across. After a while, the old bridge is a mere afterthought. It breaks away and turns into nothingness, and the new super-highway is constantly improved upon. Making way for new lanes and new travelers.

What do we do with the old bridge? Do we choose to send a demolition crew to tear it down? Or do we keep it around as a keepsake to reflect upon? Both have advantages and disadvantages, but keeping the old bridge up may allow some thoughts to steer in that direction. If the path to our new bridge becomes difficult, we may decide the old bridge is a better route once again; even though the old bridge is decomposing and dangerous to tread upon. The only question you have to ask yourself is, which bridge do you choose to travel upon?

A friend of mine created a new search engine. He was an engineer and knew he wanted to get into advertising. He wanted to directly compete with the phone book type pages, rather than the giant search engines that rule the corporate environment. Say for instance, rather than typing in "doctor or mechanic," and seeing a list of doctor's and mechanics websites, advertisements, etc... his idea was, when you type in "doctor or mechanic," a broad list of thousands would appear in front of you. His revenue would be made by the advertisements of other businesses on the pages of his search engine.

He created a vision of wanting to build wealth. This idea was his golden ticket. He knew at the end, he would be a rich man. How he would get there, required follow-though.

So, the website launched. He was so proud of his new creation. He knew this would help a ton of people. He blasted out advertisements all over every social media outlet he could find. Days turned into weeks, and weeks into months. Nothing happened.

After a week of taking some time to clear his mind, he seriously began considering giving up on his project. Determined, he decided to purchase ad space on a couple of billboards in town. He even made it a point to drive past the billboards on a daily basis with a large smile strewn across his face. He was so proud to see his advertisement displayed. He knew this would bring much needed attention to his website. This move cost him $5,000 over the course of the next month. And nothing happened.

Scratching his head, he figured, my wife and I have really nice cars; perhaps we can wrap them with advertisements for the website. He took the cars to a local print shop to have the cars wrapped. Since they were both C-Class Mercedes, he knew they would draw in a great deal of attention. Another $5,000 invested. Another month went by. Still, nothing. No new website visits. No advertising revenue in his emptying bank account.

Six months has come and gone. His website still had very little traffic. It was obvious his plans weren't working. At this point, he was acting on desperation. He went to the local radio station and purchased a few 30 second commercial spots. This investment cost him $15,000 dollars. Regardless of how frustrating this ordeal had become, he refused to give up, as he knew this idea was golden and would definitely work. Another month has passed... he even got to hear his ads on the radio a few times. So proud. Though, at the end of the day, nothing.

Nothing was working. By now, their savings was dwindling. Over this 8 month time span, he and his wife grew so very frustrated with one another. It even got to the point to where she asked him to give up on his vision. Everything they had saved since the first day they moved in together was dwindling away.

He caught wind to another idea. This one will work for certain! So he purchased a box truck, and had it wrapped. So colorful and beautiful. He even sold his car to free up extra cash and decided this would be his vehicle. It may be silly to trade in a luxury sedan for an old mail delivery truck, but he didn't care. Success was all that mattered to him at this point.

Between the sale of his car, the purchase of the old mail truck, and wrapping the old truck, he was actually able to pocket a few hundred dollars. Such a relief. So, began his daily commute from home to office and back home, with his box truck proudly displaying his new website. Well, his almost 1 year old website. Three whole months of driving his new advertisement around town... nothing.

He was out of ideas. No more tricks up his sleeve. He and his wife had filed for divorce. They had nothing left to sell. In a desperate attempt, he even asked her to sell her car so they could get another box truck to drive around town and advertise his new website. She didn't sign the papers, though she did move out. She began losing faith in her husband.

He was distraught. Sitting in his truck in a parking lot, crying away. Some people prefer to think of this as a simple action. I prefer to think of it as, he was creating new cells. Forming a new state of emotion within his subconscious body. Since he refused to give up on reaching his goals, this move of sadness and despair sent his brain into a rapid rate of search. Looking for the best possible solution in order to ease his pain and tension and fulfill his vision.

Suddenly, he had an idea. A scrolling marquee! Not just any... he was an engineer. He could build one with LEDs and make it with minimal out of pocket cost. He could put the marquee on the back of the truck! That would draw in some attention!

He began searching online for parts. He found out that he could buy 5 times the amount of parts for the same amount of money if he could fly to China and pick them up instead. Even with the purchase of the round-trip plane ticket, it still came out to be a little bit cheaper than buying the parts here in the states. He had already spent close to $30,000 in all of his attempts at success. Between the trip and the parts, this would set him back a minimum of $3000. He only had $3300 dollars left to his name.

If this didn't work, he would lose everything. It didn't matter though. He had come way too far to give up now. He made the decision, jumped on the next flight, and took off to find parts for his new advertisement.

On the plane, he mapped out his plans. He drew schematics on a notebook and figured out where every light, capacitor, and transistor would go. He knew down to an inch how much wire he would need. Rather than putting the marquee on the back of the truck, he would be able to cover the entirety of the box. He could make this truck look like a Christmas tree.

After purchasing his parts, he jumped back on the plane and came home. He was in China for less than 6 hours. There was no way he could spend any extra time, as there was not enough money for a hotel stay or even food. As a matter of fact, he hadn't eaten in days.

On the return flight... the stress was gone. The fear was gone. He knew what to do. Desperation and fear had subsided. He didn't care about his hunger. He only cared about his vision. He planted a smile on his face, and closed his eyes. He slept.

His flight arrived back home. He couldn't wait to get home and get to work. He stayed up for almost 4 straight days building his new project. Focusing on every minor detail as to not make a single mistake. He did this with a smile on his face and never let go of the idea and feeling of success. It left him for a short while, but this was his vision. He knew it would work. It had to.

The truck was finished. Days had passed and it was dusk. He needed sleep, but he didn't care. "I will just drive the truck around for a couple of hours, and then I will go to sleep." Surely, this will draw attention to my new website. "This was the answer I needed all along."

Thoughts raced through his mind about the excitement of his new truck. He managed to drive around for about an hour, but could no longer stay awake. He needed sleep. Time to go home.

The next afternoon, he awoke. He slept for nearly 16 hours. It was 3pm and he was finally getting around to making his usual pot of coffee. Rather than heading to the office today, he decided to work from home. He opened his laptop, checked his email, and there were close to 50 new emails in his inbox. "What is this?"

Did his truck work? Did his website finally have the attention he knew it deserved? Not at all. His website had still received zero attention.

His 50 new emails were in response to his scrolling marquee box truck. Pool companies, plumbers, handymen, dog walkers, babysitters. Everyone wanted to advertise on his fancy new truck! They all wanted ads of their own, just like his!

Now, his business is worth over ten million dollars! His website? No. the website was shut down, without ever having a single visitor. Now he owns a nationwide fleet of scrolling marquee advertisement trucks. Supplying service to almost 500 companies across the continental United States. He and his wife are still happily married. Their legacy has been fulfilled.

Now, ask yourself... what would have happened if he had given up? How many of us come up with an idea and go through a handful of failures before we let go of the idea and go back to the mundane life we were living before?

If you have a vision, hold onto it. Never let it go. Stay in the creative process. Stay on the super-highway of building new exits. Put up a few new road blocks. Close some lanes and reopen others. Honk and scream at the traffic. Cry, when you feel like a failure. But never, ever, give up.

A couple of years after writing that book, I understand his struggle more and more. I told that story on stage in front of thousands of people without have any understand of what he was going through whatsoever.

A movie may show someone break down in a car, or have a fight with a spouse... but they may not be aware; the struggle is part of becoming an entrepreneur. A self-employed person does a job. An entrepreneur brings a vision to life. Any and every race has a finish line, and as long as you put one foot in front of the other, you will make it.

Chapter 4
Now, everyone can build an empire.

"Let's give a simple breakdown of the three types of people you will run across when building your company:

Hourly wages are offered to *employees or contractors when tasks can be repeated multiple times, with learned effort, in an assumed period of time. These tasks can require special licenses or educational designations... they can range from a cashier to a surgeon or beyond, and their wages depend upon how many designated specialists are available in the marketplace for that particular task. You may have trouble with hourly people "milking the clock" in order to take advantage of the system, or a higher than average turnover rate if you are not offering a fair wage.

Salaries are typically offered to *employees who have combined specialties. (Managers who typically have designated education in a certain field, as well as generalized knowledge in many fields.)

Salaried employees will usually give up "rights" (freedom, time/working multiple shifts, following specific rules and mandates) in exchange for "benefits" (insurance, a consistent check, a business card, a title). These positions can be filled depending upon how many designated specialists are in the marketplace... and the wage will depend upon the stressors the person can deal with. You may have trouble with salaried people taking the system for granted, and not working as hard — as there is no time barrier. Turnover is not as common, as salaried employees will usually find a way to stay employed in order to keep their "benefits."

Commissions are offered when a contractor (sales person, entrepreneur) knows their worth, and these people typically do not need a consistent wage in order to produce income. If performance and production are the highest measurement for income, then people who work strictly on commission will offer the most value to an organization. These positions are tougher to fill, as applicants will typically need to possess "life" skills that are not taught in traditional education models... and their wage will depend upon performance and closing deals. You may have trouble with higher than average turnover rates, but if you find the right people to put on commission, you can greatly increase the chances of running a successful company – as commission only contractors are generally more useful to a company overall." – Jason Criddle, a post on Facebook.

A lot of this chapter is content from a year or so ago. I am going to update it as I read through it... but a lot of these viewpoints still hold true:

What if I told you that one of the first steps to building an empire is giving everything away? No silly, not to be broke... just a different mindset. Your money problems more than likely stem from the selfish behaviors you have exhibited that were passed down from your parents. Having watched them give up on their dreams in pursuit of staying out of debt, rather than believing something greater than their selves would eventually allow them to build prosperity had they not given up on it.

There are so many people trying to create the next fifty thousand dollar a year business... or even the next million dollar company. But they are faced with the millions of people who are doing the same thing. I decided, if I want to build a trillion-dollar business, it would only be feasible to do so by giving the trillion dollars back to the people who helped you make it.

There are a lot of speakers that will get on stage and say, "I made a million dollars, and if you follow these steps, you can do it too."

Though, not many people will tell you how hard it is. Not many people will tell you that you will be living on a couch in multiple people's homes. Not many people will tell you there will be times when you cannot pay rent or afford to eat. No one will tell you that your family will laugh at you and you will lose friends along the way. No one will tell you that it will sometimes seem as though the entire world is crumbling down right in front of you and you will feel more alone than you have ever felt in your life. No one ever told me there would be nights that I would be sitting in my shower, crying and praying to God to show me a sign and give me the power and will to succeed so I could take care of my daughter.

We have to trust in our vision. We have to know that the money, and the resources, and the people will show up at the right time. This is why I still talk to strangers... because you never know when you are going to meet someone crucial to your growth. I have met the most valuable members of my entourage in the most random of places. The strangers you talk to today will be your social media fans of tomorrow. Too many people who make a little bit of money believe they are better than other people. Without "other" people, we would not be able to build empires.

We need to let go of the idea and mentality of being a "know it all." I remember days of proclaiming a title of being a jack of all trades. Which immediately introduced me to the other half of the equation... being a master of none. We have so many weakness as leaders. Recognition of these faults allows us to grow. By recognizing our faults, we can then delegate those responsibilities to other leaders that have weaknesses in areas where we excel, and yes, these people could very well be sacking your groceries, or serving your food at your favorite restaurant.

We must surround ourselves with those who complement our skills. We are all born leaders. Our organism is in constant search of balance for basic survival. We have lost our basic abilities of belief, leadership, and creation because we have externalized these processes and given the power to other people. If you take a moment to look around you, everything you think you could possibly need to survive, is around you. We have created the perfect environment to distill creation. We have created people with job titles that we call them teachers and leaders... which then leads us to believe we do not have the means within us to teach or lead others, or even ourselves.

We think of ancient civilizations as primitive cultures. Could it be so, that these civilizations were so far advanced, both intellectually and spiritually, there was no reason to externalize such forces in other forms of technology. As a matter of fact, what we actually do know about pyramids, is that they were used as chambers to grasp the power of the sun, moon, and stars, and magnify the internal forces each and every one of us carry within us to this day.

We are all born artists. We are all natural singers; merely having forgotten how to do so because of the abundance of self-proclaimed bullshit we have filled our heads with. But, if we one day recognize we indeed have the gift of pitch and we can sing, then we can definitely learn to become better with practice. I was born with the ability to draw. And the times in my life where I became better, were the times when I was focused on strengthening that particular skill. I know I still have it in me, but it is a gift I am choosing not to work on at this time. To spend time focused on drawing would be time spent not focused on the path I am on now. Our strengths and our shortcomings make us who we are, and we all have the ability to lead. To build empires. Being the person needed to build an empire takes practice as well, and if you believe you can build one... you can.

Try this simple experiment... fold your arms in front of you, like normal. Is your left arm laying across the top of your right? Or the right across the left? Now, try to fold them the other way. The other way? Yes, pretty awkward isn't it? Keep in mind, neither is wrong, but for you, this is "normal". This is your way, and this is what you are good at. If you can grasp that simple concept, you will come to the realization that no one in the world can cross their arms the way you can cross your arms. No one in the world can compete against you or offer the world what you can offer.

I heard this saying once... find a person doing what you want to do and emulate and copy them to become successful. When I first heard this, I wrote it down on a sheet of paper. After a few minutes of examining the quote, I drew a big circle around it and crossed a line through it similar to the no-smoking sign we all know and love. Underneath it, I wrote, "Realize no one can do what you can do. Do that, to become successful."

We spend far too much time thinking about competition. People will get a license or a certification, and not only do they head out and immediately copy every single detail of the other entrepreneur, they worry that the other person somehow operates on the same playing field. They have more ideas. They work longer hours. They have an edge.

In reality, the only competition you will ever face, is yourself. You don't have to worry about the sales person down the street. You must worry about your lack of creativity. Your lack of ambition. Your lack of passion and desire to excel or build a more prosperous future. A legacy.

There is a bit of absurdity when it comes to competition. Some people believe we are in a dog eat dog world. Some people believe survival of the fittest is the law that rules the land. When society took Darwin's approach to survival out of the fittest from a book and spread rumors about a famous man's perception, they forgot to mention that the very same book only mentioned survival twice, and the word "love" more than 90 times.

In actuality, abundance and cooperation through democracy rules the land. Take a look at a tree. A bird. A lion. A grasshopper. A humpback whale, or a blade of grass. All of these being are accepting of abundance. And all of them, never stop working. None of them.

When you see a school of fish all turn directions at the same time, or a flock of birds gracefully pulling off the same maneuvers in midair, it may seem to you like a bit of magic. What you don't see with the naked eye are the birds voting for a direction. Once the 51st percentile decides to turn on a dime, they all turn together. Or the 51st percentage of fish... or even the dear that are grazing the field, and eventually head towards their choice of watering hole for nourishment. You would think the "alpha male" would be making the decisions for the group, and if you are thinking so, you are wrong.

Most animals, if resting, are restoring energy from their last attempt at a hunt, or their most recent flee from a predator. Perhaps, a fox just spent a good part of his day digging holes, a beaver building dams, or a lioness chasing down a zebra for her children to feed. These animals all accept life and death. They all follow the passions and desires to fulfill their purpose. Even if from the outside, we feel their purpose may be one of cowardice, one of humor or even misunderstanding.

This is where truth comes into play. Truth does not have to be understood to still be truth. People get stuck believing their religion may speak truth, not realizing, truth is the greatest religion of all.

Do you ever think animals ever stress about their work? Do they ever take days off, or sleep in on Sundays? Or argue with their spouses about jealousy or money problems?

Ah… money problems. Because we humans have to pay to live. And, we are the only ones walking the planet that must do so. So, why is it so difficult to live in abundance? Or even fathom living in abundance? Why is it so easy to build something great when all of nature and everything around you seems to just, be?

Poverty is a mindset too. All around you is abundance. You may say to yourself, "The world is running out of food and water." More food can always be grown. More trees planted, more streams and rivers cleaned. More can always be made, fixed, planted, or created. You can create anything you put your mind to, and it only takes a decision.

One may say, "I have a mountain of bills to pay. I am always out of money and I will never get ahead." We are never in lack. People will think they are running out of money, not remembering they get paid in 5 days. But even saying the words, "I am running out of money," cast a spell over your thoughts and internal condition.

How many times are you repeating to yourself over and over…? "I will never make it. I can't do it. I can't afford it. I a fine with my subpar car. I am fine living in this cruddy apartment. Money doesn't grow on trees."

The first time I made a vision board, I wrote, "I will have $1,000,000.00 by my 31st birthday."

Then I started dreaming. Over the course of days, weeks even, my goals started changing. I began having more realizations of my purpose. More thoughts and new opportunities were surfacing because I finally took the time and effort to align my thoughts with my intentions.

There were new additions to my goal board, almost daily. Good thing I bought a dry erase board. It must have changed at least 30 times over the course of 3 months. At first I wanted a private jet. Then I wanted to own an airline. At first, I wanted to go to law school. Eventually, I dreamt of owning a law firm. The most significant change, was the dollar amount. Not because of want of more items for myself, but I began questioning as to how much I could really change the world with a million dollars. What could I really change with a billion?

Rather than asking for money, you have to think to yourself what you can give to the world that is worth that amount of money. You can dream and say out loud all you want that you need millions of dollars to reach your goals, but what are your goals? Why do you want to build an empire? What are you going to do with your millions of dollars? How many lives are you willing to change? How many friends and how much sleep are you willing to lose to obtain it? How much are you willing to create just to turn around and give it away?

If I indeed wanted to build an empire, it was going to take a whole lot of giving away, which was going to take a whole lot of creating. The funny thing was, all I had under my sleeve with that realization – was a couple of hundred bucks from a network marketing company, and a single manuscript that I was working on. Fast forward to now, and I can see what my path has made me. I sit here now, a man who is ready to run a million, billion, or trillion-dollar company. Of course, I skipped a lot of my story but the idea is still the same. At the end of all self-help books… at the end of manifestation practice, is the person, the spirit, the divine soul you became to achieve your goal.

Market yourself.

We learn from ideas and mistakes, and if you learn these lessons from other people, even better. Ideas cannot be stolen. Why? Because ideas are meaningless without action. If someone tells me about something they are going to work on in the future, more power to them. If it can make my company or image stronger and I am willing to take action right now, more power to me. All manifestation practices aside, you still need action. Thought or faith without action will not get you far. What if I had visualized The Smartr App, but didn't build it? No amount of prayer would have made it fall into my lap. I still would have a process to endure to get there.

I could tell you my future plans all day long, but rest assured, you don't have my knowledge, my past, or my work ethic. I don't worry about sharing my ideas with people because people are not me. Just as I am not them. And without them, I could not be me; and the other way around. That said, if you have a worthwhile idea, and you are willing to tell me all of the intricate details about it while sitting on your ass and doing nothing with your life, don't be upset when you see the idea played out. And that isn't just me, it's with anyone. If I were to share an idea with someone more willing, capable, with a better approach and more assets available to them than I have, it was my fault for sharing. Especially if I were not willing to do anything about my idea to begin with. Get the picture?

Marketing in its truest form is to work on becoming the person you were born to be, and you should be marketing yourself each and every moment of every day. Making eye contact with people, shaking hands, striking up conversations with absolute strangers, go above and beyond your call of duty by ways of one simple word, communication. People in general do not communicate with one another anymore. It seems easier to win the lottery than it is to get someone to look at you or say a simple, "hello," or "thank you." Just because people aren't willing to take these steps for you does not mean you should not be willing to take the steps for you. I mean, them... wait, no, I mean you.

On Martin Luther King Day of 2014, I was waiting at the local chain coffee shop with my business partner and her son. I do not drink coffee, however, we were waiting for a gentleman who owned an internet broadcasting company and wanted to speak with me about being on a few of his radio stations. Our meeting was scheduled for 11. Naturally, we arrived 15 minutes till and began to wait.

After making a couple of phone calls and sending texts, we decided, at 11:15 to walk across the parking lot to this amazing hole in the wall sandwich place. They serve breakfast and lunch, and later in the week, I was pleased to learn they served dinner as well. I had been there before, and of course, this time I appreciated the ambiance quite a bit more. I always take note of how efficiently a restaurant is running, especially during busy time periods. It shows how effect the management is with their employees – and I always look forward to a moment of greeting a manager and talking with them about how well they are running their place of business. I do this with most places I go, but there is something special about a place that puts a good meal in your belly.

There was room in the restaurant for about 70 people. I would venture to guess there were 50 or so guests patronizing the business on this day. Stood in line, ordered our meals, went to our table, and received our food. We even began talking a little bit of business strategy when the phone beeper. He sent a text proclaiming he had just arrived at the coffee shop and we were not there so he was going to leave.

We tried calling him again and he sent us to voicemail. Then he sent a text saying he was going to play golf and if we needed his services we could meet with him at his office later in the week.

Now, keep in mind, we were early. Not late. We waited. Went somewhere within walking distance. Stayed glued to our phones. And even tried to invite him to lunch. What did I do? I shrugged it off! Surely this will be a time for an even better opportunity! And guess what? It was!

We finished our meals and I decided to guy purchase a couple of cookies for us. And, of course, for my little princess at home. When I got back to the register, I took a quick mental photograph of the 50 cookies laying in the presentation tray on the counter – then glanced over my shoulder and noticed there were still about 50 lovely people, chatting away and enjoying their lunch.

My heart began to pound. I told the girl I wanted to purchase all of the cookies, which of course, took her by surprise! She began counting them when another associate come over to help her box them up in a few foam to-go containers. The manager, being the alert fellow he was, came over to assist his employee. He looked at me and asked if I would like to keep the presentation tray they were on. It seemed there are not many times someone purchases all of the desserts at one time.

Now my heart is beating out of control. It almost feels like the chest cavity has been broken and now my beating heart is freely slapping against my shirt. I tell him who I am and begin talking about my foundation. I told him I am going to interrupt the restaurant and tell them the meaning of Martin Luther King Day. After words, I will shower them with cookies. I generously asked him if he minded. He shook my hand, we exchanged business cards, and he exclaimed he did not mind at all.

When that happened, I had not yet learned of future and past self, or about the vortex which is created by both. Our past self is the self which is usually ridden with fear. It does not progress. It often procrastinates, lacks ambition or energy, and it will talk you out of your dreams. The future self wants you to succeed. This is your God-realized, trust self, who has already achieved all of the abundance and success you are experiencing right now. I did not know that interrupting a restaurant to give them cookies would have so much bearing on who I was... nor did I have any idea that it would lead to more public outbursts on my part, which then led to more opportunities. I used to think marketing was simply holding up a sign. Nope... that is advertising. Marketing is giving your product away. If you are your product, market the shit out of yourself.

Trainer to Trillionaire 2.0

Assets, marketing, value, faith, universal laws and principles. I have heard so many people say becoming a millionaire will teach you a lot about yourself... the millions of dollars are not where the value lies either. The value lies within the person you become on the path to making millions of dollars for yourself.

When I wrote my first book, I was a guy with a lot of dreams. Well, now, I still am... but I am a God-realized man who works diligently to reach his goals. One who understands the value of assets. One who found out worth and value does not lie in money, but the self. Faith in God and the universe necessary, but even it is useless without action.

I really think becoming a trainer taught me how to become a man. And working towards this path to build a trillion-dollar company has led me to God. My action is supported by my faith, which is supported by my action. If you wish to become a millionaire, and you don't reach your goal... don't give up. Just make a bigger goal.

Having Emma unleashed a creative force in me. Her walking led to my losing weight and becoming a coach and nutritionist. Coaching led to building confidence, telling my story, and becoming a speaker. Fueling my speaking circuit led me to sales and network marketing... which led me to trying to always fix a system that I always knew could be easier. To me, getting a prospect to buy into my MLM was just as easy as walking up to someone for a few seconds, and exchanging bits of information over the phone. So, I created a piece of software that does just that.

I build a trillion-dollar company, because I decided a long time ago to give a trillion dollars away. People can finally build assets for themselves by exchanging a few words, and a number on a cell phone. The Smartr App will change the world forever... and it is not just an app; it's an investment tool – and it will buy people the freedom they need to thrive.

Today.

Today, I am thankful... for each and every day. I will be better every day. I will do more every day. I will greet each day with laughter, love, and gratitude, and say goodnight with a brief reflection of the day's events before I honor my creator for the gift of today. This day was given to me, and should not be taken for granted. I need to concentrate on living in the now, but I will momentarily reflect on the day's events for the sole purpose of seeing what I can improve upon before the sun rises tomorrow and my eyes close tonight. When given the choice to do nothing and take action, I will forever choose to take action. The person who used to do nothing is gone. If this person reappears, I will become aware, take action against them, forgive myself, and move on. TODAY, I TAKE ACTION.

Today, I will become wiser. I will choose to absorb knowledge and educate myself in every subject matter possible, as my thirst for wisdom is a primary driver in my success and freedom. I will condition my body and eternal spirit to make peace with the only enemy I thought I had... my mind. I have spent far too long fighting what I thought was a never ending battle, but not anymore. It is impossible to defeat an enemy that only exists within me. I have no enemies... I have no failures... only opportunities for growth and expansion. TODAY, I GROW. TODAY, I EXPAND. TODAY, I AM WISER.

Today, I will win. Tomorrow I will win. For the rest of my life, I will win. I will be successful. I will be great. My rewards and wealth are a byproduct of the value and service I offer those around me, including myself. The lives I change are my true reward... My success is a byproduct of the lives I change, as well as my decision to change myself. My life is my reward. TODAY, I AM SUCCESSFUL. TODAY, I AM GREAT. TODAY, I WIN.

Today, I overcome. I shall suffer no longer. I will not waste my energy on long-term goals. I will break my long-term goals down into simple daily steps, and instead, devote my energy to becoming the person I must become to reach my long-term goals. Yesterday, I was not that person. Today, I am that person. I am stronger than yesterday; mentally, physically, emotionally, and spiritually. I have not only adapted to, but have overcome the thief that robbed me of fulfilling my destiny yesterday… my mind. TODAY, I AM STRONGER. TODAY, I OVERCOME.

Today, there is no enemy. Today, there is no fear. Not anymore. I am the only thing that has ever stopped me, but today, I forgive myself. I forgive everyone I feel has ever done me wrong, simply because, no one has ever done me wrong. At the time they performed actions which I thought were against me, or wrong, I did not understand myself the way I do now. I can show them compassion, pray for their healing, and hope one day we can sit side by side while I share with them how grateful I am for every breath they take. TODAY, I FORGIVE.

Today, I un-focus. Sometimes people will focus their anger towards me, but I will not focus my anger towards them. I am in control of my feelings, my emotions, and my actions. Only I can make the choice to become upset or angry, and I no longer make that choice. I forgive them. I forgive myself. Pain is necessary, but my suffering is optional. Today I make the decision to never suffer again. TODAY, I AM IN CONTROL.

Today, I realize my purpose. My body belongs to me and so does my mind. And now, I am now in control. This magnificent and beautiful vessel was created for one thing and one thing only… my purpose that God has given me. My destiny that I now realize. It is said that the two most important days of our lives are the day we are born, and the day we realize WHY we were born. For me, that day is today. TODAY, I AM MY PURPOSE.

Today, I make the decision to be wealthy. I make the decision to be healthy. I make the decision to be successful. I make the decision to have a smile on my face even when no one else is smiling. I make the decision to provide for those who cannot provide for themselves. I make the decision to stay in control of my mind. I make the decision to forgive even when I am not forgiven. Today is my purpose. Today is my gift. Today, I am in control. TODAY, IS MY GIFT. TODAY, I TAKE RESPONSIBILITY FOR MY LIFE.

Today, God will move mountains for me, because today, I will move mountains for God. TODAY, I AM READY.

Chapter 5
Jobs are bullshit when the only payoff is money.

In truth, just about everything is bullshit when money is the only payoff. I remember being invited out to an investor meeting that was taking place in DC... I actually went to a few of them, but I learned a very valuable lesson on that first trip, when the VP of the firm told me, "Do not take on any investor who can only offer money." At the end of the day, they will not be worth your while... and if someone is not willing to provide you with support, resources, man-power, education, etc., then you do not need them. I promise you.

When starting The Smartr App project, I had already gained funds for Smartr Pills, the network marketing company which preceded the idea for the app software. Since I had already gained funds, I never imagined I could visit some of the same investors with a better idea and receive even more money. Of the dozen or so investors I brought on board, absolutely none of them offered me anything more than support; which was needed and appreciated at the time. Only a couple of them got to the point to where they stopped offering support as well. One of them got to the point to where she began personally attacking me, my motivations, and my ethics. Another just decided to pull out her money at the last minute – friends of the one who personally attacked me.

To follow the story you read in Understanding Manifestation, some people give up. Some people are not willing to change their minds, or shift directions at the last minute. Some cannot cope with change, delays, or improvisation. They give up right before they strike gold, right before they build a giant sign on their box truck, or they pull an investment out right before a trillion-dollar company launches. Now, had either of these investors had more to offer than money, we would have never gotten to the point we did. There would have been no one pulling money out, or getting upset at testing delays... if I wasn't getting upset, they should not have either. I was the one in the thick of it, after all. All they had to do was sit back, and collect a check later. And now, their lives will remain what they were before... and the same anger and impatience that caused them to leave The Smartr App Company before launch will follow them throughout the rest of the decisions they make. Unless they are willing to change of course. Everyone can change if they want to. That's why you are reading yet another book from me. And I am sure you have made quite a bit of money from my app too.

The same goes with jobs, one night stands, or fast food. It always sounds like a good idea until you realize there is no payoff on the other end. I have said a few times, "we should fear being successful at something that doesn't matter," and it still holds true. If you are not following your purpose or passions... if you are just waking up to collect a paycheck... then it is time to wake the fuck up and ask yourself what you are doing.

Values precede valuables, and what one holds valuable in their life is directly correlated to the amount of value they are able to offer to others. Someone who is not living in the house they want, not driving the car they want, not getting on a plane to go wherever they want, simply has not brought enough value to other people's lives. Their value and worth would match their values/valuables and net worth. I am sure you have some idea inside you that is worth money. And not just money, a life worth living. The money will come to you if you have a worthy reason for it. It's time we all take a long look at our lives and ask ourselves, "am I chasing a paycheck, or a dream?"

If you need investment dollars to follow your passion, or if you are working a job you could care less about... are you chasing a paycheck, or a dream? Most of life is bullshit when the only payoff is money. There is no value in money... the value is in you. How valuable do you want to be?

Today.

Today, I am thankful... for each and every day. I will be better every day. I will do more every day. I will greet each day with laughter, love, and gratitude, and say goodnight with a brief reflection of the day's events before I honor my creator for the gift of today. This day was given to me, and should not be taken for granted. I need to concentrate on living in the now, but I will momentarily reflect on the day's events for the sole purpose of seeing what I can improve upon before the sun rises tomorrow and my eyes close tonight. When given the choice to do nothing and take action, I will forever choose to take action. The person who used to do nothing is gone. If this person reappears, I will become aware, take action against them, forgive myself, and move on. TODAY, I TAKE ACTION.

Today, I will become wiser. I will choose to absorb knowledge and educate myself in every subject matter possible, as my thirst for wisdom is a primary driver in my success and freedom. I will condition my body and eternal spirit to make peace with the only enemy I thought I had... my mind. I have spent far too long fighting what I thought was a never ending battle, but not anymore. It is impossible to defeat an enemy that only exists within me. I have no enemies... I have no failures... only opportunities for growth and expansion. TODAY, I GROW. TODAY, I EXPAND. TODAY, I AM WISER.

Today, I will win. Tomorrow I will win. For the rest of my life, I will win. I will be successful. I will be great. My rewards and wealth are a byproduct of the value and service I offer those around me, including myself. The lives I change are my true reward... My success is a byproduct of the lives I change, as well as my decision to change myself. My life is my reward. TODAY, I AM SUCCESSFUL. TODAY, I AM GREAT. TODAY, I WIN.

Today, I overcome. I shall suffer no longer. I will not waste my energy on long-term goals. I will break my long-term goals down into simple daily steps, and instead, devote my energy to becoming the person I must become to reach my long-term goals. Yesterday, I was not that person. Today, I am that person. I am stronger than yesterday; mentally, physically, emotionally, and spiritually. I have not only adapted to, but have overcome the thief that robbed me of fulfilling my destiny yesterday... my mind. TODAY, I AM STRONGER. TODAY, I OVERCOME.

Today, there is no enemy. Today, there is no fear. Not anymore. I am the only thing that has ever stopped me, but today, I forgive myself. I forgive everyone I feel has ever done me wrong, simply because, no one has ever done me wrong. At the time they performed actions which I thought were against me, or wrong, I did not understand myself the way I do now. I can show them compassion, pray for their healing, and hope one day we can sit side by side while I share with them how grateful I am for every breath they take. TODAY, I FORGIVE.

Today, I un-focus. Sometimes people will focus their anger towards me, but I will not focus my anger towards them. I am in control of my feelings, my emotions, and my actions. Only I can make the choice to become upset or angry, and I no longer make that choice. I forgive them. I forgive myself. Pain is necessary, but my suffering is optional. Today I make the decision to never suffer again. TODAY, I AM IN CONTROL.

Today, I realize my purpose. My body belongs to me and so does my mind. And now, I am now in control. This magnificent and beautiful vessel was created for one thing and one thing only... my purpose that God has given me. My destiny that I now realize. It is said that the two most important days of our lives are the day we are born, and the day we realize WHY we were born. For me, that day is today. TODAY, I AM MY PURPOSE.

Today, I make the decision to be wealthy. I make the decision to be healthy. I make the decision to be successful. I make the decision to have a smile on my face even when no one else is smiling. I make the decision to provide for those who cannot provide for themselves. I make the decision to stay in control of my mind. I make the decision to forgive even when I am not forgiven. Today is my purpose. Today is my gift. Today, I am in control. TODAY, IS MY GIFT. TODAY, I TAKE RESPONSIBILITY FOR MY LIFE.

Today, God will move mountains for me, because today, I will move mountains for God. TODAY, I AM READY.

Chapter 6
The Smartr App for a better life.

Yes, I believe in my software, and yes, I believe the new industry we created will change the way the entire world does business. Sometimes people just need a push from someone who is willing to change the status quo and sacrifice everything along the way. For what? To help seven and a half billion people who have no idea I exist. Yet.

As I sit here, in the final day before launch, designing marketing materials with my buddy Marko who has become an asset in and of himself, I smile. I smile because I know I did it. Building this company has been the most difficult thing I have ever endured from a business standpoint. And being an entrepreneur, every single decision I have made in the last 6 months has been made with The Company in mind... and every single one of those decisions has effected every other part of my life. Hence, being an entrepreneur. Unlike employees or even the self-employed, entrepreneurs do not get any days off. No vacations. No lunch breaks – well, until the finish line is crossed.

I became a trainer because I wanted people to feel the same feeling I had felt the day I compared two of my before and after pictures. I started a publishing company because I wanted people to feel what I had felt the day I held my first book in my hand. I enjoyed teaching people MLM because I wanted people to feel their first commission check in their hand, the way I did. I spoke to thousands, because I wish someone had spoken to me the way I had spoken to them... at the time I needed.

I started The Smartr App Company, because I believe the veil of lies that has been cast over us for so long is breaking. I believe the world is coming to a realization that people do not need jobs to survive. Artists can be artists. Singers can sing, plumbers can... plumb?

One of the books I was working on some time ago was all about network marketing – and I still believe it to be an answer for some... I said, "every entrepreneur should have network marketing in their arsenal." After spending some time earning commissions from a few companies, and helping people build teams in others, I made the decision that any self-employed person should be involved in MLM. It just made sense. We spend so much time marketing ourselves, that regardless of what we decide to do to make a living, we should also carry with us as many sources of income as we possibly can. Books, MLM, underwater basket weaving skills...

Of course, my perception has changed a bit. Now, I believe every entrepreneur should have a few Smartr Apps in their phone, with a Smartr Bnk Card in their back pocket. Every person who wants it, now has a tool in their pocket that can build assets and create passive income. And once enough people start using the app, it will become an idea... then, it will just be.

If you were to face multiple cameras at the same fish tank, from different points of view, anyone watching the monitor may think he is looking at many tanks of many different fish. After a while, he may begin to realize, he is in fact looking at the same fish, with many different perspectives of the same tank. If you were to back out of your mind, and take a long look at the entire world, no matter which set of eyes you look through – you would soon realize, we are all looking at the same thing. We are all doing the same thing. Climbing towards the same thing... The reason The

Smartr App is already successful, is because, I am you. And you are me. We are doing the same thing.

We are doing the same thing, no matter which set of eyes are looked through. I believe the world is coming to a realization that people do not need jobs to survive... and I believe they will soon be free of these shackles which have tied them down for so long. And a big ass part of it, is The Smartr App. It is the only thing that makes sense to me. I created the app, because the world needed it. The world created me, because it needs my ideas. The world needs me just as much as I need them, and I need everyone as much as they need me. No matter which set of eyes are looked through, we are all ascending towards God. How do I know? Because I am here. I am doing it. And I am going to teach everyone how. Today, and every day.

Today.

Today, I am thankful... for each and every day. I will be better every day. I will do more every day. I will greet each day with laughter, love, and gratitude, and say goodnight with a brief reflection of the day's events before I honor my creator for the gift of today. This day was given to me, and should not be taken for granted. I need to concentrate on living in the now, but I will momentarily reflect on the day's events for the sole purpose of seeing what I can improve upon before the sun rises tomorrow and my eyes close tonight. When given the choice to do nothing and take action, I will forever choose to take action. The person who used to do nothing is gone. If this person reappears, I will become aware, take action against them, forgive myself, and move on. TODAY, I TAKE ACTION.

Today, I will become wiser. I will choose to absorb knowledge and educate myself in every subject matter possible, as my thirst for wisdom is a primary driver in my success and freedom. I will condition my body and eternal spirit to make peace with the only enemy I thought I had... my mind. I have spent far too long fighting what I thought was a never ending battle, but not anymore. It is impossible to defeat an enemy that only exists within me. I have no enemies... I have no failures... only opportunities for growth and expansion. TODAY, I GROW. TODAY, I EXPAND. TODAY, I AM WISER.

Today, I will win. Tomorrow I will win. For the rest of my life, I will win. I will be successful. I will be great. My rewards and wealth are a byproduct of the value and service I offer those around me, including myself. The lives I change are my true reward... My success is a byproduct of the lives I change, as well as my decision to change myself. My life is my reward. TODAY, I AM SUCCESSFUL. TODAY, I AM GREAT. TODAY, I WIN.

Today, I overcome. I shall suffer no longer. I will not waste my energy on long-term goals. I will break my long-term goals down into simple daily steps, and instead, devote my energy to becoming the person I must become to reach my long-term goals. Yesterday, I was not that person. Today, I am that person. I am stronger than yesterday; mentally, physically, emotionally, and spiritually. I have not only adapted to, but have overcome the thief that robbed me of fulfilling my destiny yesterday... my mind. TODAY, I AM STRONGER. TODAY, I OVERCOME.

Today, there is no enemy. Today, there is no fear. Not anymore. I am the only thing that has ever stopped me, but today, I forgive myself. I forgive everyone I feel has ever done me wrong, simply because, no one has ever done me wrong. At the time they performed actions which I thought were against me, or wrong, I did not understand myself the way I do now. I can show them compassion, pray for their healing, and hope one day we can sit side by side while I share with them how grateful I am for every breath they take. TODAY, I FORGIVE.

Today, I un-focus. Sometimes people will focus their anger towards me, but I will not focus my anger towards them. I am in control of my feelings, my emotions, and my actions. Only I can make the choice to become upset or angry, and I no longer make that choice. I forgive them. I forgive myself. Pain is necessary, but my suffering is optional. Today I make the decision to never suffer again. TODAY, I AM IN CONTROL.

Today, I realize my purpose. My body belongs to me and so does my mind. And now, I am now in control. This magnificent and beautiful vessel was created for one thing and one thing only... my purpose that God has given me. My destiny that I now realize. It is said that the two most important days of our lives are the day we are born, and the day we realize WHY we were born. For me, that day is today. TODAY, I AM MY PURPOSE.

Today, I make the decision to be wealthy. I make the decision to be healthy. I make the decision to be successful. I make the decision to have a smile on my face even when no one else is smiling. I make the decision to provide for those who cannot provide for themselves. I make the decision to stay in control of my mind. I make the decision to forgive even when I am not forgiven. Today is my purpose. Today is my gift. Today, I am in control. TODAY, IS MY GIFT. TODAY, I TAKE RESPONSIBILITY FOR MY LIFE.

Today, God will move mountains for me, because today, I will move mountains for God. TODAY, I AM READY.

Chapter 7
The art of not giving a shit.

The last couple of weeks that I lived in my mom's rent home, while waiting for the app to launch, I moved a desk into the garage. It is where I am sitting now while finishing up this rough draft. I needed a little quiet in order to get this thing finished.

There are a few doors sitting up against the west wall of the garage, with a work bench next to it. Since my mom decided to remodel parts of the house, the garage has been sprinkled with pieces of the once old bathrooms and kitchen – so now there are also these doors out here which came from the hallway. Just sitting; waiting for paint. I took a big fat marker and wrote at the top of the door:

3 Steps for Trillionaire Success!

1. Don't give up or give a shit.
2. Do it for God/the world.
3. Repeat.

Now… I did add a step to that list, but the one that may stick out to most is – Don't give a shit.

On my left hand I have tattooed, "I must not tell lies." While many people recognize the line from Harry Potter, they assume I have the message tattooed on me simply because I am a Harry Potter fan. I must admit, I will get down with some Order of the Phoenix anytime of the day, but I am a bigger fan of the message. And not even about lying to others… as I think that is a given. My life changed when I stopped lying to myself.

I must not tell lies.

I remember writing my first book and listening to the advice of so many people who had never authored a book... nor had they achieved any form of substantial success. I felt the same way as I did when kids at school laughed at my new, very large, plastic frame glasses. I shaved my head because I thought people hated at my afro. I played games in my spare time, I absolutely became bored to death with school, and even though I never found myself attractive, I somehow captivated the imaginations of the ladies then, just as much as I capture full audiences now. I cared too much about what other people felt... and at the end of the day, I was simply lying to myself; just to be the person other people wanted me to be.

It wasn't until I spelled out "Bad Mother Fucker" on my business cards that I finally began to realize, I am who I am, and that person is the same person in business as he is in his personal life. One day I stopped lying to myself – I stopped caring about what people would think when I would say certain things – I started living my life for my daughter and my true self, and I just plain didn't give a shit anymore about people's opinions.

I know that I walk with purpose and live on purpose. The afro that I began growing 8 months ago has turned into dreadlocks. The black, plastic-framed glasses that I wear now are even larger than the ones I hid away in school. I still don't have a college degree even though I have written more books than most people will read in four years' curriculum. I still play games in my spare time, I still have all of the attention from the ladies, and I never apologize. Every single action I take is predetermined and expected, simply because – I know where I am headed. My finish line does not have me living by other people's standards... it has me recreating standards, and helping to change and rebuild the world for better and for always.

I spent so damn long living my life for other people... then one day, I started living for myself. Living smarter. And you should too. If you decide to follow through on a decision which could ultimately build a legacy for you and your family, it will be hard. And I promise you, it will get worse before it ever gets better. All you can really do is have faith. Believe in yourself. I am not going to say "stay positive," because negativity, anger, regret... it is all necessary for growth. Stop lying to yourself, and just be the person that you already know you are.

Today.

Today, I am thankful... for each and every day. I will be better every day. I will do more every day. I will greet each day with laughter, love, and gratitude, and say goodnight with a brief reflection of the day's events before I honor my creator for the gift of today. This day was given to me, and should not be taken for granted. I need to concentrate on living in the now, but I will momentarily reflect on the day's events for the sole purpose of seeing what I can improve upon before the sun rises tomorrow and my eyes close tonight. When given the choice to do nothing and take action, I will forever choose to take action. The person who used to do nothing is gone. If this person reappears, I will become aware, take action against them, forgive myself, and move on. TODAY, I TAKE ACTION.

Today, I will become wiser. I will choose to absorb knowledge and educate myself in every subject matter possible, as my thirst for wisdom is a primary driver in my success and freedom. I will condition my body and eternal spirit to make peace with the only enemy I thought I had... my mind. I have spent far too long fighting what I thought was a never ending battle, but not anymore. It is impossible to defeat an enemy that only exists within me. I have no enemies... I have no failures... only opportunities for growth and expansion. TODAY, I GROW. TODAY, I EXPAND. TODAY, I AM WISER.

Today, I will win. Tomorrow I will win. For the rest of my life, I will win. I will be successful. I will be great. My rewards and wealth are a byproduct of the value and service I offer those around me, including myself. The lives I change are my true reward... My success is a byproduct of the lives I change, as well as my decision to change myself. My life is my reward. TODAY, I AM SUCCESSFUL. TODAY, I AM GREAT. TODAY, I WIN.

Today, I overcome. I shall suffer no longer. I will not waste my energy on long-term goals. I will break my long-term goals down into simple daily steps, and instead, devote my energy to becoming the person I must become to reach my long-term goals. Yesterday, I was not that person. Today, I am that person. I am stronger than yesterday; mentally, physically, emotionally, and spiritually. I have not only adapted to, but have overcome the thief that robbed me of fulfilling my destiny yesterday... my mind. TODAY, I AM STRONGER. TODAY, I OVERCOME.

Today, there is no enemy. Today, there is no fear. Not anymore. I am the only thing that has ever stopped me, but today, I forgive myself. I forgive everyone I feel has ever done me wrong, simply because, no one has ever done me wrong. At the time they performed actions which I thought were against me, or wrong, I did not understand myself the way I do now. I can show them compassion, pray for their healing, and hope one day we can sit side by side while I share with them how grateful I am for every breath they take. TODAY, I FORGIVE.

Today, I un-focus. Sometimes people will focus their anger towards me, but I will not focus my anger towards them. I am in control of my feelings, my emotions, and my actions. Only I can make the choice to become upset or angry, and I no longer make that choice. I forgive them. I forgive myself. Pain is necessary, but my suffering is optional. Today I make the decision to never suffer again. TODAY, I AM IN CONTROL.

Today, I realize my purpose. My body belongs to me and so does my mind. And now, I am now in control. This magnificent and beautiful vessel was created for one thing and one thing only… my purpose that God has given me. My destiny that I now realize. It is said that the two most important days of our lives are the day we are born, and the day we realize WHY we were born. For me, that day is today. TODAY, I AM MY PURPOSE.

Today, I make the decision to be wealthy. I make the decision to be healthy. I make the decision to be successful. I make the decision to have a smile on my face even when no one else is smiling. I make the decision to provide for those who cannot provide for themselves. I make the decision to stay in control of my mind. I make the decision to forgive even when I am not forgiven. Today is my purpose. Today is my gift. Today, I am in control. TODAY, IS MY GIFT. TODAY, I TAKE RESPONSIBILITY FOR MY LIFE.

Today, God will move mountains for me, because today, I will move mountains for God. TODAY, I AM READY.

Chapter 8

Becoming your true "self" is a bag ass part of success, believe it or not.

I have a pretty cool book coming out later this year about The God Theory... which is my own theory about the path and transitions a God-realized person goes through in this life. Even though you might think your spirituality, and becoming who you are meant to be might not have much to do with the circumstances of your life, they surely do. Working on the self has nothing to do with physical reality, circumstances, addictions, meditation... none of that; all you have to do is realize the "I AM," in you. Being the amazing person you were born to be is all you have to do. That has nothing to do with actions... it has to do with decisions. The person you are meant to be does not need to-do lists, or management, or even motivation, because the person you are meant to be, is God; and God decides to be successful and creative every day. Just look outside.

I don't cover the app in this chapter, I just wanted to provide you with some damn good reading. Enjoy.

Patience

Our patience comes from understanding the present moment is what we have. Can you remember five minutes ago? Can you fathom what life will be like five minutes from now? This moment, right now, takes forever. It is all we can really comprehend. And 'right now' can last for mere seconds or ages depending on what we have going on in our environment or our minds.

Einstein theorized that time must change according to the speed of a moving object relative to the frame of reference of an observer. We call this the Theory of Relativity, or more notable for this example, time dilation. Many have tested this theory through experimentation; proving, for example, that an analog clock ticks more slowly when traveling at a high speed than it does when it is not moving. For example, you can take two synchronized clocks, and send one of the clocks on an airplane trip around the world at a high rate of speed. When observing both clocks after they meet back up, you would find that the traveling clock now reads an earlier time than the clock that remained stationary. The closer you travel to speed of light through space, the less you age, or experience change in time. This is called "time dilation."

I remember being in Crossfit in the middle of a WOD and having that huge clock on display right in front of us. We used the equation of power to calculate our workouts. Power = force x distance/time. Performing 30 reps of a 200-pound deadlift in three minutes would not produce as much power as performing the same amount of reps with the same amount of weight in two minutes. You don't just get stronger by performing exercises based on weight, you also become stronger by performing exercises based on time. I would often tell my clients, "You got 22 seconds stronger today." That being said, whenever we were in the middle of a workout, we perceived time to be moving at a slower rate than through the relative perception of sitting still, or performing any other actions in life. We were literally so focused on moving as fast as possible, our perception of time seemed to slow down. Counteract this with someone who would be watching the competitors workout, the clock would actually be moving faster for them in comparison to someone who was not observing or competing at all. What time dilation teaches us; it is impossible to say whether or not two events occur at the same time when they are separated by space or perception thereof. This is also the reason why even a short flight somewhere seems to take foreeevvveeerrr.

The page you are looking at now to read this very sentence is literally, physically not the same page you were looking at once you started reading this page. The only reason it may seem is because your perception of the page has not changed. The time variable of the page has yet to produce enough recognizable difference; therefore, you experience the continuity of it being "the same old" page. The perception of "the same page" is a self-created illusion based on your perception of this moment, and your mental and emotional connection to this moment. You know the person you are today is not the person you were five years ago. Likewise, the person you are now is not the person you were a millisecond ago. Your illusion of time is created through the appearance of a similarity of connecting moment to moment. Since so much of our reality looks the same from moment to moment, it makes us "feel" like it is. Just as the way we walk down the street, this continuous physical movement perpetuates our illusion of a timeline, when in reality, we are only living in one ever-changing moment.

This feeling of continuous momentum is not real. Our awareness of the dimension creating these experiences is an illusion we are creating. Because we only experience now, whatever has happened or will happen is no longer real either. Consciousness, and its explanations to our "self" is all that of exists of the events that take place in life. In reality, our consciousness is also responsible for our falsified lineal description of an observable continuous experience.

We also perceive time through the changing mechanics of a clock even though it is not actually measuring time. The way a clock works is no different than counting with your fingers. Nothing is being changed except your perception of reality. Even our circadian rhythm (sleep cycle) or our observation of the planet orbiting around the sun does not measure time either. Our perception of day and night are timeless, just as the Earth's orbit around the sun are timeless as well. In fact, if you were to leave the atmosphere of the planet, you would no longer experience a sunrise or a sunset and you would therefore have no realization of a measurement of time. Within our own illusion of time, our experiences appear to lead from one to another. This experience does not exist anywhere else.

I met an FBI profiler a couple of years back, and he asked me what I thought was one of the fundamental processes holding humanity back from evolving spiritually. I told him that our ideas of the Earth's orbit could be one simplified mechanic, as we are taught about this pie plate, circular dynamic in elementary school. We all remember the diagram of there being a sun in the "middle" of our solar system, and all planets are in a perfect orbit, spinning on a level axis around the sun. In actuality, this revolution would create a reality like that of the movie, Groundhog's Day, where the same day would be played over and over again. Except, this 365 Earth day revolution would create a year that is played over and over again. If you really think about it, isn't this what is actually happening in the minds of most of us?

In reality, at the equator of the planet, we are spinning at over a thousand miles per hour, and chasing after the sun with a forward speed of over 66,600 miles per hour. By chasing, I mean, that is pretty close to the speed at which the sun is traveling through our ever expanding universe. If you think about an outstretched slinky, this is the helical pattern our planet follows as it is trying to catch up with the electromagnetic current of the sun, which we call gravity, and all of the planets in our solar system are following along on the same path. Without even bearing regard to the laws of light and motion, we are never sitting still. When you are on an airplane traveling at 500 miles per hour, it feels like you are sitting still. When you are sitting in your chair at home, you even feel like you are sitting still... in reality, we are constantly chasing something, which could mean, we should always be chasing something.

It is difficult for most to cope with the idea of there not being any "time." Right now is the only moment we can, have, and ever will experience throughout our lives. All ideas, change, perception, and any parallel phenomena will only exist in the awareness of one ever-changing moment, which we call time. Time is nothing but a concept of observation we have created to comprehend what we experience in our specific conscious state of being. If one person's consciousness is out of focus with another's state of awareness, it will seem as though the people perceive and live within multiple realities all at one. This is one of the barriers I typically come up against in communicating with certain people, because my own mental and physical disposition towards reality would not be considered to be – what most would call "normal." The idea of parallel universes and parallel timelines or timelines is composed of an individual's experience of time.

Conscious reality has no specific rate of change, but what we experience does. It would not make sense to define how fast reality changes, because it is a moot point, as time is only an illusion. All we actually can measure is what changes within our own individual reality, and we create that awareness upon how we quantify the change of a specific experience. Because time is only an illusion, motion does not technically exist either. However, that can be an entire topic or book on its own, which would require new definitions of the relationship between light, space, time, matter, gravity, and magnetism... as well as giving new parameters of what you may consider to be "definitions" of those specific terms. Sufficive to say, we will use the terms speed and motion for now.

The observation of light (electromagnetic energy) through space and time define our awareness of physical perception. This is how God observes physical reality through us. Just because we cannot visually "see" the teleportation rate of light (appearing and disappearing) throughout fractions of specific moments, does not mean it does not happen that way. We cannot see radio waves, but we can hear the radio. We cannot visualize Wi-Fi, but we can get online. We cannot so the sun's ultraviolet rays, but they still affect your skin. How we observe moments of the movement of light, or electromagnetic energy, determines change in an individual's reality, by observing the movement of light. The speed of light (299,792,458 meters per second – 186,282.4 miles per second – 1 Planck Length) determines how we perceive changes in consciousness from moment to moment, as well as from person to person. Our brain is indeed involved in our awareness of change, but those changes are specific to our subjective state awareness as well as the elemental properties that compose that experience.

So, what the heck is a Planck? Planck originated through physics, and Max Planck's' theories of dimensional analysis typically ignore "normal" factors. While there is no reason to believe exactly one Planck time has any special physical significance, we still use Planck time to represent a rough time scale at which quantum gravitational effects take place. All scientific experiments and human experiences happen over billions of billions of billions of Planck times. The outcomes of those experiments and the exact time scale at which they become observable is represented through Planck Time. A Planck length is the shortest distance physically possible, and motion is a way to express the teleportation rate across this length in space and time. A Plank length is about one point six, times ten to the minus thirty-fifth meters. Plank time is a natural unit of measurement used to measure a specific amount of time, similar to milliseconds, but a much smaller amount of time. One Planck time is about ten to the minus forty-fourth seconds, or .00000000000000000000000000000000000000000001 seconds. Unlike our typical units of measuring time, Planck times are considered "natural" because they are defined by physical constants, like gravity and light.

Planck time is not a representation of how fast the brain works to create consciousness, it is simply measuring how fast our physical world within our brains exists and changes. One Planck time is how long it takes for physical matter of the universe to change, and the human brain requires quadrillions upon quadrillions of Planck times to create the experience of one specific moment in time. When you think of it this way, it shows you just how slow the action potentials of neurons really work. It will also show you the infinite possibilities of parallel timelines when you realize all of these measurements are based upon the experience of just one person's consciousness, so the speed at which the brain experiences these measurements are irrelevant, as that perception will be significantly slower than Planck time to Planck time. That is because what we perceive is the changing of Planck time to Planck time, not necessarily how fast we subjectively perceive a moment changing.

While saying something as simple as shooting a bullet from a gun takes about 1 second, we could also say it took over 18 and a half tredecillion Planck times (tredecillion is ten to the seventy-eighth power). If you placed one million Planck lengths across the diameter of a penny every second, it would take over three hundred and seventy-three quintillion years (373,512,604,720,230,000,000 years).

"All matter originates and exists only by virtue of a force, which brings the particle of an atom to vibration and holds this most minute solar system of the atom together.

We must assume behind this force the existence of a conscious and intelligent mind. This mind is the matrix of all matter." – Max Planck

Once you start moving closer to the realm of God, time literally does not exist in your reality anymore. Could it be because your body and mind are moving at such an exuberant rate of speed that common anomalies like time and space hold no bearing to your perception? Could this be why you seem to know certain events are going to happen long before they happen? Could we postulate that your feelings of déjà vu stem from the fact that you have actually left your body through dreams or imagination and traveled to and observed an event before your body had a chance to catch up with the situation in "real" time?

I taught my daughter to sit back and enjoy the ride because of the age old question, "are we there yet?" When she was a little younger, she would sometimes say things were far away. Or driving to a particular mall or museum took a long time. I would explain to her, it only takes a long time if you are being impatient. It isn't that it takes a long or short time to get somewhere, it just takes time. If you accept the fact that things take as long as they take, you never have to worry about feeling impatient.

We should be patient with our jobs, our dreams, our children... did I say dreams? How many times have you had an idea that would completely change your life? How much energy and time did you devote to this new found chance before you gave up on it? A day? A week? Maybe a few months?

When I wrote my first book, I figured simply writing the book would make it become a best-seller. I even had some stalkers that were bashing me online and telling me and others that the book was a joke and it would never go anywhere. A few weeks passed. Then a few months. I took the book everywhere with me. I would keep copies in the truck of my car. I carried boxes of them with me to seminars. I sent free digital copies with just about every single email I would send to anyone just to help the book gain traction. There were many times where I felt discouraged, but rather than falling off the horse and giving up on my goal, I decided to rewrite it. Re-launch it with a new cover and a few changes to the content to make it look better on the shelf. While I was busy with the new launch, I wrote another book and launched some short eBooks which I turned into a compilation for the new paperback.

About this time, a major publisher called me and offered me six figures for my first book. I was taken aback. I didn't know what to do or how to respond. I spent many hours on the phone with the publishing representative as well as a couple of partners I was involved with in my business. I received so many differing opinions and I had no clue who to listen to. Them, or myself. Finally, I picked up the phone and called my buddy Ron Brackin – a well-known author on that little list we like to call, New York Time's Best-Sellers.

We had a long conversation about publishing with a large publishing house vs. self-publishing. We had a long talk about how writing is a gift that is given to us by God and we have to ask ourselves, are we writing to make money, or are we writing because we are supposed to?

There had to be a reason this publishing company called me. What did I do with my book that made it so special? Obviously, I had been patient enough to let the book gain traction. It made its rounds to someone important and word got out that it was best-seller worthy. Since Ron had more knowledge than anyone on the topic, I took his opinion a little higher into consideration. His suggestion was to stick with my self-published book.

After doing more research, I realized that after having read thousands of books in my life, I had written a book with a best-selling formula. It was completely by accident too. After learning of this formula, I looked at the books I had just recently written and realized I wrote them with the same concepts. I came to terms with the "why." Why did the publishing company offer me money? Because I knew how to write gold. Do you know what happened the very next day? Another publishing company called. Then another in the very same day.

I later found out that a literary agent had been forwarded a digital copy of Trainer to Trillionaire and sent it to the publishers that she thought would enjoy the book. This had taken place just days beforehand. After listening to the company's offers, reviewing contracts and agreements, and sitting down and thinking for a few days, I decided to start a publishing company. All I thought was, "If I can write a best-seller, I can teach other people to write them too."

If at any point I had given up on my dream, I wouldn't have started my publishing company. Which led to the consulting company. Which led to the marketing company. Which led to my alternative lending firm. Which led to my fifty plus global brands. Which lead to the children's books published by my company... other authors, and even this book you are reading now.

There were times throughout this whole journey when I felt like giving up and getting a regular job again. Anytime I was ready to throw in the towel, I would have to remind myself that everything happens on God's time, not mine. All I have to do is be patient and the answers will come to me. The more actions I take towards my future, the less time it will take to achieve whatever it is I am trying to achieve. A debunked version of the theory of relativity was right there in front of me. The faster I move, the faster the clock ticks. Boy this stuff gets confusing.

I have told many before... I don't consider myself to be a motivational speaker. When I talk, I tend to piss people off. But getting pissed off at myself led me to where I am today. I got tired of living a mundane life and going absolutely nowhere. Sure, I had a successful pool business at one point, but I could no longer stand it. It wasn't my purpose. After it crashed, I gained more weight than I had ever gained in my life, and walked around with an angry look on my face and a heart filled with regret and hate. After Emma started walking, I learned a kind of patience that is still incomprehensible to me.

A lot of "motivational speakers" will tell you the story of making a million dollars, or trying to tell you to follow your dreams so you can make a million dollars... not many people will tell you the truth about following your dreams. Making a dream come to life is really fucking hard. There are going to be times you don't eat. You will have to live in motels and starve while you watch your child(ren) eat. There will be times where you want to give up. People will laugh at you and hate on you. You will lose friends and some of your family will stop talking to you. But you have to ask yourself how bad you want your dream to come true. So, how bad do you want it?

Have you ever been dreaming... and in that dream, you found a thousand dollars and put it in your pocket, just to wake up and find out it was a dream? Yeah... it sucks. But it can really happen. You just have to be patient enough to see it through.

Health and Balance

I am sure if you are reading this, you have read both Breaking Through and Breaking Point. Breaking Through was an eBook that I placed inside Breaking Point, which was a compilation of a few of my eBooks.

I sit here in the beginnings of 2015, getting fit again. I just ate about four pounds of some very delicious chicken with my family that I made for lunch. Two breasts and four thighs with my secret recipe. Right before I prepped them and put them in the oven, I went into the driveway and did 108 lunges with 100 pounds on my back. It was a nice six-minute sweat session. It felt fantastic. Not my workout for the day, just a workout. I still need to go to the gym tonight after the sun goes down.

I have been a yo-yo dieter throughout my life, but it wasn't until Emma started walking that I really took time to learn about health, nutrition, food, and how to take care of the human body. I still make quite a few mistakes, and I am working ultra-hard now because I took the last eight to ten months off from being fit.

I worked out a couple of times a week in that time. Hell, who am I kidding...? I worked out whenever I felt like it, and sometimes a week or two would go by before I saw the gym again. We had a gym in our apartment at the time, but I found myself doing as little as possible to get by when it was empty. When New Year's Resolution time came around, I too walked into a big box gym to renew my old membership. It was time. I pretty much have my business setup in full automation mode and my life is pretty damn great. Emma is with me 24/7, my mom lives close by so she can watch after Emma when I have any kind of important meetings, I am wealthy, I am enjoying getting healthy again, I have great friends, I am becoming even closer with my family, my books are selling and gaining recognition like crazy... I won't say, "It couldn't be better." It always can, but I am not going to complain.

Complaining is what seems to take me out of balance. Complaining is what makes me work against myself and my goals. There are no bad decisions to be made on this realm, but complaining and/or having a negative attitude or negative perspective certainly will draw you away from gathering up the energy needed to accomplish whatever it is you are trying to accomplish.

I didn't care about my body most of last year. I say that I had more important things on my plate, but in reality, I disregarded my health. In Breaking Through, I spent a brief moment of my perspective on over-eating, or binge eating. I spoke of us not necessarily wanting the food, rather, we are recreating the feeling eating the food creates. At the time, I had a solid idea... but it took writing a moment of clarity, which lead me to writing this section.

I was over at my mother's house for dinner. My little sister lives with her, and my daughter happened to be with me. I had to run a few final errands right at dinner time, and when I got back, I wanted to get in a garage workout before eating. Even after my, at home ass kicking, I kept fielding phone calls. Needless to say, I was going to be eating this meal alone.

My mom cooks some award winning dishes. She taught me how to use the kitchen, which is a very safe place for me. I realized, the best meals are cooked with love, and the more you talk to and caress your food, the better the meal.

Think for a moment about your favorite meal at your favorite restaurant. I would almost guarantee, you would pick it over a fast food meal, any day of the week. Why? The lack of quality in the ingredients? The feeling of guilt and shame that immediately follows? What you thought would be gratification from your unhealthy meal, immediately turns into a decision filled with regret. You wish you could take it back, but low and behold, you made the decision. It is time to think about why you did it.

On this particular night, she made a fabulous meal. One she used to make when I was a child. Since we grew up without much money, our meals usually consisted of cheap carbohydrates. Lots of starches, lots of sauces, gravy, breads. And of course, there is nothing wrong with eating this way. It is only a matter of having an understanding of why one would eat this way. It wasn't until later in life I learned of proper nutrition, so when I come across meals such as this, thoughts of balance always come into play. My conditioned trainer's mind strategically places carefully served portions onto my plate. And there is a feeling of pride associated with not over indulging on the meal.

But, I went back for a second serving. It was ground beef, cream gravy, and white rice. There were a lot of macronutrients in there my body could use... but seriously, I knew this wasn't a well-balanced meal. I wasn't trying to kid myself.

Then, something crazy happened. I went back for a third serving. I scooped it on my plate, without even thinking. The feelings of nostalgia had completely taking over my mind and body processes. I, at this point, started shoveling the food into my mouth. I switched from rice, to white bread. Food I would never have in my own home, but you know how it is when you are at mom's.

I actually went for a fourth serving. The second, third, and fourth were nowhere near the size of the first, and as I said, the decision had already been made. So, I wiped my plate clean with my fourth slice of bread. I must have consumed 500g of carbs. And it dawned on me, what I had been doing.

My eye caught the corner of a cereal box. I immediately began conjuring up memories of sitting down to eat a bowl. After I made the decision to be a healthy person, I had created habits of having a bowl of cereal, then putting my bowl in the sink. But, it wasn't a mere decision. It was a change in consciousness at that point in my journey. Actions were being taken, based on completely different rules here.

Here I was, overeating uncontrollably. I realized the kid was back. I became the 8 year old, unstoppable, garbage disposal of a child. I remember scooping out a plate of food which could satisfy a king. I did it with so many meals. Throughout my childhood, I was known for drinking a gallon of milk a day, and eating two, or sometimes three times the serving size of my siblings. Why not? I saw my father do it.

My body and mind was in search of a balance. I was eating smaller and smaller servings, and as I thought about, the servings were equaling up to the amount of food that would have been on my plate, over 20 years ago. Not only were the feelings of nostalgia in full effect in my thought process, there were hormones of pure, sweet indulgence coursing through my very veins. I was not satisfied. I had to eat until it felt my stomach would burst. I had to eat until it hurt.

A great mentor once said, "The best ideas of man are lying dormant in the graveyard, never to be known to the world." I am paraphrasing of course. He is putting emphasis on the fact that too many people spend way too much time talking and not enough time acting. Maybe it is because they are not aware they have the ability to change this cycle.

I have said it before, but I will say again... anything I ever talk or write about is coming from my very own, very limited perspective.

Take a moment to do research yourself. I don't for a moment believe everything that is told to me. As a matter of fact, I love being proved wrong. I love the opportunity to be wrong. I have also learned we have a scary gigantic majority population of people who believe things that are not true and are performing conditioned behavior and do not know why.

We were told to eat huge servings of grains on a daily basis – which caused a couple of generations of diabetes, cancer, coronary heart disease etc. – and it was because grains were a commodity that could be stored and big bucks could be made off of it. We are told a house is an asset. Yeah, for a bank! But we are not told that. We are never told what really goes on when a house is sold – we are just mimicking the behavior of everyone else.

My perspective, however, is based upon spending the majority of my life learning from as many people's perspectives as possible. Not just befriending people and getting to know them – learning why they made the choices to live their lives. What was the "why" behind their actions? Were they paying attention to their lives? Were they living for themselves or living in someone else's cycle? Were they willing to change in order to have what they wanted?

This year, I decided that I will not turn back. Regardless of what is going on in my life, I will never make the decision again to disregard my health. I would spend so much time thinking about what it took to lose all of the weight I had lost before; all of those pushups, all of those burpees, the days upon days in the gym, and it would demotivate me. I was so involved with the thoughts of the stress it would put on my body, the sweat, the pain... I was forgetting how much fun I actually had being in shape as well as the energy and pain it took to get there. Working out two to three times a day for almost three years was so fun at the time, but since I had fallen out of my regimen, the idea of starting once again was driving me nuts.

Then reality hit. I didn't start out working out that much... I started out enjoying the beginning of the process. I started out feeling crazy excited when I saw pictures of my body changing in the mirror. I don't have to go balls to the wall right now, I just have to get started. Not to mention, training was one of the best parts of my life. It introduced me to public speaking, some really great people, behavior and excuses in other people – which of course – led to writing a few books and being about to talk to people about decision making. My decision to get healthy and become a trainer eventually led me to the wonderful life I live now. On top of learning of so many people and so many careers, I was able to learn about myself and my own limitation.

I have discovered, now more than I ever have before, our energy doesn't come from food or water. It comes from making decisions. Right now, I am writing this book... which I know for a fact will become an immediate best-seller. I have had this book outlined for a few months. I have done hours of research. I have had video and audio transcribed so I could read and reread it again. I have slept with headphones in, as affirmations, books on tape, and hundreds of speeches and lectures from ridiculously intelligent scientists, speakers, and mentors were absorbed into my parietal lobes while my eardrums banged away in my sleep.

As much as I have studied, I kept telling myself I was not ready to write. As much as I have accomplished in the last year, it seems my life is getting even better even faster simply because I am making my body healthier again. Most of the greatest things in my life happened to me at the healthiest point in my life. It is all connected. It's all balanced. I won't get very far into weight loss, or muscle gain, or nutrition; you can read about that stuff in some of my other books. Even then, you still need to get help from a professional or two. I will however, share a blog post with you that I posted when I decided to get my ass back into the gym. It's called: It's good to be back.

I spent most of last year writing and not lifting. It's so funny that I used to tell my clients they had to make time for the gym and I found myself not making time. I still worked out with my buddy (and old client) Kent twice a week... but my two to three times a day, seven days a week disappeared from the moment I stopped teaching Crossfit at Camp Hero Fitness. Soon after I went back to my old Rec Center to train, I decided to stop training all together and started pursuing writing and speaking, and building my companies.

Of course, New Year's always brings on those feelings and desires for change. So, I did what any 31-year-old man would do... I got a gym membership. I did workout at my old apartment gym, but it wasn't the same as being in a gym. Not for me at least. Not at this time of my life. I realized I would go to my apartment gym and do as little as possible to work up a sweat. Psychology teaches us, we perform better at something we are good at when we have a crowd. We perform worse at something we do not have knowledge in when we have a crowd. This could explain why people without gym knowledge feel "naked" when they first step into one. One thing I can assure you is, no one is watching and no one cares that you are there UNLESS you believe they do.

I felt so alive during the middle of a WOD, and I feel that feeling again. I pretend the crowd is mine, and it keeps me fired up and motivated. Thanks to muscle memory, within the next 30 to 60 days, I can be in better shape than I was before. I miss the atmosphere of Camp Hero Fitness… where we were almost forced to get better. Everyone was watching you. Change wasn't necessarily expected, but it was encouraged. If they weren't so far from me now, I would definitely go back. I can't wait to see their new location by the way. If you do stop in, say hi to Justin, Darius, Adam, Jayme, Kyle… all of the old crew. I believe Brett and Lance are still training in the area as well.

A few tips I can give someone for the New Year…

Eat for your muscle. – So many people are afraid of gaining muscle or "getting big." I can assure you, Arnold didn't get that way on his Bowflex for 15 minutes, 3 days a week. Take in an adequate amount of protein so your muscle can grow. Every single calorie you burn on a daily basis is dependent upon the amount of muscle you have on your body. If you aren't building muscle, you are burning muscle. Period.

Think before you eat. – Becoming consciously aware of your food choices is crucial. A few months ago, I wouldn't think twice about shoving a dessert m=in my face or going to Taco Bell at 2 in the morning on the weekends, simply because it was a simple decision to make. Now that I am becoming healthier again, I don't even have cravings for dessert or fast food. All I want is fresh fruits and vegetables and fresh sources of protein. My desire for water has increased and I find myself snacking on eggs and cheese rather than crackers, chips, and cookies. There is this saying, "the mind craves what the body needs." It is making sense to me now more than ever.

Drink a lot of water. – I used to be able to tell when my clients didn't get enough water in the day… simply because they weren't performing at their peak. Water carries nutrients, water keeps you limber, and water gives you the energy to keep going. Most of us blame lack of food for lack of energy. It is usually lack of water.

Energy comes from decisions, not food or water. – If you are feeling tired or worn down, go to the gym. Your decision will work up the motivation to work out, and you will feel great while you are there and after you leave. Often times, we find ourselves lying in bed in the morning, trying to get a few more minutes of sleep. If we would just put our feet on the floor, we would have ample energy to get up and start our day. Did that new found energy come from food? Or did that new found energy come from making a decision?

Learn what you are doing, or hire professional help. – I have a video available in my university, as well as a couple of chapters I have written in books called, Go after Proven Results. Don't hurt yourself in the gym, and don't waste time in there either. Baby steps are just that, baby steps... if you want to make real changes, know what you are doing. If you don't know what you are doing, get help. I have seen way too many people go to the gym for a year and not get half of the results of someone going for 30 days that either has help or knowledge. Do not hire a trainer based on their cost... hire a trainer that is able to get you results. How do you know if they can get you results? Easy... have they gotten anyone else results before?

Get a partner or join a team. – If you are looking for real motivation, surround yourself with people that won't allow you to give up. If your friends or family aren't doing anything to change their health, you will usually hear nothing but negativity from them. Who cares? Just find someone who will keep you positive. This will usually be your trainer. Join Crossfit, get a partner with similar goals, or even join a basketball or softball team, or a spin class. People with the same goals typically won't allow you to quit. And, since you are the average of the 5 people you spend the most time with, your life will probably change for the better all the way around anyway.

Don't give up. – Just about anything with consistency will change your body, regardless if it is weight training or eating cheeseburgers every day. Most people give up too soon... on EVERYTHING. I even had a lady tell me the other day that she tried positive affirmations for a whole week before she stopped. Why? "Because it didn't work." – Her answer. I have spent my whole life working on myself and I sure do not plan on giving up yet. You could have very well found gold if you had only dug another inch or two... You are too special and too beautiful to give up on yourself, and your past doesn't have to be your future. Make a decision and become who you want to be. It really is as simple as that. Remember, you are not fat... you just have fat on your body. You are love and God's ultimate creation. Believe in yourself.

Am I missing anything? Oh yes...

Cardio burns calories, not fat. – All of that cardio you are doing can go against your goals. There is nothing wrong with cardio, but you have to ask yourself what your goals are. If you are trying to get fit, lift. If you are trying to become a better runner, lift and run.

If you haven't subscribed to my blog at jasoncriddle.com, you should take a moment to do so. I can't promise you I am blogging every single day, but I do like to share some ideas. Now that I am getting back into the fitness realm, I am sure I will be sharing nutrition & lifting tips and techniques periodically, rather than just writing about business philosophy, behavior, theology, physics, and squirrels.

How do I become wealthy anyway?

I used to wonder what the difference between wealth and riches were... then I experienced it. Riches are money. Wealthy is what is left when there is no money... or the byproduct of the money. The "who" and "what" you have become. The "where" you live. The "how" you got to that point. Far too many people focus on making money, when they should focus on giving value to others.

There is an entire truckload of wealth and riches just around the corner, just waiting for you. Yes, you. What are you going to do to get it here, and what are you going to do to make it show up? Rather than worrying about making money, you should be thinking about how you can make other people money. How can you enrich other's lives? What, of yourself, can you offer to the world to make them change the entire way they live and experience the world?

Steve Jobs did it. Mark Cuban did it. Einstein did it. Edison did it. Whether they were rich or wealthy, you know of their names because of the actions they took and the decisions they made that changed your life, not theirs. The most successful and wealthy people to ever walk this earth created their own careers. So, what are you doing? Are you trying to become a member of society? Or are you trying to become your best self?

If you are focusing on trying to get a career with a title that a million other people share; if you are trying to pass a course with fifty other people in your class, with another class of fifty waiting to walk in after you, while that class is being taken in a thousand schools all across the country, be prepared and stop to look around. There is your competition right there. Waiting for you to fuck up so they can snatch the rug right out from underneath you.

But what about you? Your beautiful self? What about the God that God put within you? What about that passion that you have the NO ONE on this planet can do except you? You know it's in you. You were doing it yesterday. You were complimented on it last week. This morning, someone told you how great you were at it, and you should do it for a living. So, why aren't you doing it?

Are you afraid? Is your amygdala causing a little too much cortisol to be released into your bloodstream because of your unfamiliarity with the unknown? Are your friends laughing at you and telling you that it's a stupid idea and you shouldn't do it? Did it try it before for a few months and you were too damn patient to see it through? Did you happen to read the section about patience and not giving up on your dreams?

Your way to wealth is to provide value to others. The law of compensation. A little law that I have written about many times which states your will be compensated for the amount of value you bring to the world around you. Money and wealth is the byproduct of your value. A byproduct of your service and contribution. This doesn't mean you have to work your ass off doing something you hate. As a matter of fact, your passion should be the exact opposite. You should not only love what you are doing to become wealthy, but you would want to teach others to do it, pay others to let you do it, and be willing to die happily while you are doing it. Your path to wealth creation exists within you. All you have to do is make the decision to become the "you" that God put you here for.

Today.

Today, I am thankful... for each and every day. I will be better every day. I will do more every day. I will greet each day with laughter, love, and gratitude, and say goodnight with a brief reflection of the day's events before I honor my creator for the gift of today. This day was given to me, and should not be taken for granted. I need to concentrate on living in the now, but I will momentarily reflect on the day's events for the sole purpose of seeing what I can improve upon before the sun rises tomorrow and my eyes close tonight. When given the choice to do nothing and take action, I will forever choose to take action. The person who used to do nothing is gone. If this person reappears, I will become aware, take action against them, forgive myself, and move on. TODAY, I TAKE ACTION.

Today, I will become wiser. I will choose to absorb knowledge and educate myself in every subject matter possible, as my thirst for wisdom is a primary driver in my success and freedom. I will condition my body and eternal spirit to make peace with the only enemy I thought I had... my mind. I have spent far too long fighting what I thought was a never ending battle, but not anymore. It is impossible to defeat an enemy that only exists within me. I have no enemies... I have no failures... only opportunities for growth and expansion. TODAY, I GROW. TODAY, I EXPAND. TODAY, I AM WISER.

Today, I will win. Tomorrow I will win. For the rest of my life, I will win. I will be successful. I will be great. My rewards and wealth are a byproduct of the value and service I offer those around me, including myself. The lives I change are my true reward... My success is a byproduct of the lives I change, as well as my decision to change myself. My life is my reward. TODAY, I AM SUCCESSFUL. TODAY, I AM GREAT. TODAY, I WIN.

Today, I overcome. I shall suffer no longer. I will not waste my energy on long-term goals. I will break my long-term goals down into simple daily steps, and instead, devote my energy to becoming the person I must become to reach my long-term goals. Yesterday, I was not that person. Today, I am that person. I am stronger than yesterday; mentally, physically, emotionally, and spiritually. I have not only adapted to, but have overcome the thief that robbed me of fulfilling my destiny yesterday... my mind. TODAY, I AM STRONGER. TODAY, I OVERCOME.

Today, there is no enemy. Today, there is no fear. Not anymore. I am the only thing that has ever stopped me, but today, I forgive myself. I forgive everyone I feel has ever done me wrong, simply because, no one has ever done me wrong. At the time they performed actions which I thought were against me, or wrong, I did not understand myself the way I do now. I can show them compassion, pray for their healing, and hope one day we can sit side by side while I share with them how grateful I am for every breath they take. TODAY, I FORGIVE.

Today, I un-focus. Sometimes people will focus their anger towards me, but I will not focus my anger towards them. I am in control of my feelings, my emotions, and my actions. Only I can make the choice to become upset or angry, and I no longer make that choice. I forgive them. I forgive myself. Pain is necessary, but my suffering is optional. Today I make the decision to never suffer again. TODAY, I AM IN CONTROL.

Today, I realize my purpose. My body belongs to me and so does my mind. And now, I am now in control. This magnificent and beautiful vessel was created for one thing and one thing only... my purpose that God has given me. My destiny that I now realize. It is said that the two most important days of our lives are the day we are born, and the day we realize WHY we were born. For me, that day is today. TODAY, I AM MY PURPOSE.

Today, I make the decision to be wealthy. I make the decision to be healthy. I make the decision to be successful. I make the decision to have a smile on my face even when no one else is smiling. I make the decision to provide for those who cannot provide for themselves. I make the decision to stay in control of my mind. I make the decision to forgive even when I am not forgiven. Today is my purpose. Today is my gift. Today, I am in control. TODAY, IS MY GIFT. TODAY, I TAKE RESPONSIBILITY FOR MY LIFE.

Today, God will move mountains for me, because today, I will move mountains for God. TODAY, I AM READY.

Chapter 9
Don't give up

I can tell you from experience, more than anything else... the only thing you really have to do in order to achieve your goal is DON'T GIVE UP. Abundance is waiting for you, and as long as you are focused on building value in yourself and others, you will make it. The mind will always find what it is looking for... and any bullshit you have to deal with along the way is simply part of the process. Enjoy some more content from Understanding the God Theory.

Abundance is waiting.

Earlier I said that your path to wealth is by offering value to other people's lives. I also compared riches vs. wealth for you. So what is the difference between wealth and abundance? What is abundance? Where are you right now?

Look inside the home you are sitting in. the restaurant, mall, hotel room... wherever you are, take a moment to look around. Go look out the window for a moment; what do you see? Do you see houses? Apartments? Trees? Cars? People? Or do you see abundance?

Take the typical fruit tree. What if an orange tree was made by man? The tree would probably have ten or so oranges. They would be processed and imperfect. You would have to pay taxes to get to the tree. The oranges would more than likely be at the very top branches, and guarded by people with guns, to ensure only the top 1% were able to get to the orange.

Now, think about God's orange tree. It starts as a seed, absorbs the nutrients it needs to thrive, grows strong roots without question, and sprouts more fruit than anyone would need. There are thousands upon thousands of oranges brought upon the branches over the life cycle of one single tree. And it will product this fruit for its entire lifecycle. Not only will it produce this fruit, the fruit that falls that is not consumed by those that need it, will reabsorb into the earth to provide more vitamins and essential nutrients for the tree. The flowers will produce pollen which the wind will carry to give life to other plants around it. Seeds will fall into the ground to produce more seeds which will produce more fruit. The tree is a perfect example of abundance. The tree trusts God. God trusts the tree.

What if we trusted God, because I assure you, God trusts us. Our bodies were made to last forever. We poison them with alcohol and processed food. We make decisions that stress our minds and cause us to grow old faster than we are supposed to. We think of getting sick, which causes our bodies to get sick. We have access to the same energy, nutrients, and elements that the orange tree has available to it, but we choose to not trust in God. We choose to ignore the laws beset before us which allow us access to our dreams and the life we desire to live. We choose to be lazy. We choose not to believe. We choose to make conscious decisions to live with regret, pain, fear, depression, anger. We only think the Law of Attraction exists if we read a book to help us understand it, even though the Law of Attraction has been working for us throughout the entirety of our lives.

The Law of Attraction is in action every second of every day, and it is composed of the matter which you are carrying in your mind. Your thoughts are real. Not only are they measurable forms of energy, they are more real than this life you live which you call existence. You wake up every day and do the same thing over and over while your mind runs wild and free. The experiences which cross your mind the most are what your reality becomes, whether you are aware of the thoughts or not. Everything you know about life started in your mind. Just as everything you see before you started in someone else's mind, be it man or God. God created us, and we try our best to destroy God. Most of us will try harder each and every day to pick our own and everyone else's lives apart so that we can live poorly, miserably, and in complete sadness. We live to die. We live to have our dreams be nothing but dreams rather than creating the reality we really want. We allow fear to keep us from creating our own abundant existence because we don't want to be considered different. We want to conform and be like everyone else. We would rather be accepted by losers than ignored by them. We would rather conform to a simplistic idea of normalcy rather than being extraordinary. We are mean, defiant, crude, selfish, jealous pieces of shit for the most part. Until, we make the decision to change.

Creating abundance is as simple as becoming abundance. When I look out my window, do you know what I see? Abundance and love. I see the creative force of love which was needed to build my home, to create the dirt my home sits upon, and the love it took to give birth to the persons that built my home. Love did all of this, and it is all around you. Abundance is everywhere.

Can you count the stars in the sky? Or the grains of sand on a beach? Or the leaves in the tree nearest you? Probably not. But I am sure you can count the dollars in your wallet, the pieces of clothing in your closet, the cars in the parking lot, and the number of songs on your mp3 player. I bet you cannot count the number of times you became angry just last week, but I assure you that you can count the amount of times you have been in love throughout your life. Why? Because you take so much for granted and do not pay attention to or believe in what does.

We should spend our time focused on love and abundance. We should trust ourselves and our ability to give to others without question. We should let people cut us off in traffic without reacting. We should hold open doors without a thank you. We should give our last dollar to a beggar because we know there is no such thing as a last dollar. We become abundant by believing we are equals to God. We are equal to the grains of sand, the leaves, or the dollars in our wallet. Once we give love to what matters, love will be given to us by any and all elements of the universe. Stop thinking about how much money you want, and start believing dollars want you.

By simply wanting, you will not have. To want, means you are without. To say you want a million dollars means you do not have a million dollars. You can say it as many times as you like, and the more you say it, the further away it becomes. You apply negative thoughts to everything else, and your negativity continues to fuel your desire of lack, which is the figurative million dollars. Rather than wanting the million dollars, become the million dollars. What would you need to do to become a million dollars? What kind of person do you need to be for a million dollars to find you? What should you be willing to give and give up to acquire that million dollars?

And of course, money is just an example. If you want to have the best friends, you must become the best friend. If you want to have a loving spouse, you must become a loving spouse. I remember being in a relationship with this beautiful girl year back, and I could have sworn she loved her dog more than she loved me. Whenever she would come home, this bond of light between her and her dog shined brighter than the sun. This was years before I was in true control of my own mind, so I responded as any weak person would respond, with jealousy. As I grew wiser, I realized what was actually happening.

The very moment she walked in the room, whether after being at work for an entire day, or being gone for a few mere minutes, her dog greeted here with love. More love than I had ever been willing to give. Her dog would run around and circles, and lick, and jump, and be aroused with pure excitement at the sheer sight of her owner. The more I became aware of this bond, the more beautiful it became to me. And the more attention I began to show my girlfriend. I wanted to be showered with the abundance of her love, so I became an abundance of love. The only thing that ended this relationship was a career change which separated us, but I will never forget what happened the day I learned to become an abundance of what she needed, rather than always thinking of my needs.

We can have abundance as soon as we become abundance. All we have to do is let go and trust in God. We have to become the tree, the sand, the stars, the love... the universe. As it is forever expanding, we should be forever expanding. There is no death around you, there is only life. There is so much to go around, that if we all had a moment of clarity and decided to stop being selfish, we would indeed have any and everything we could possibly desire.

Try something for me. Think today about something you really want. As soon as you realize you are no longer thinking about it, think about it again. Try to hold onto it as long as you can. Keep repeating the thought in your mind about what you are, not what you want. I am love. I am rich. I am abundant. I am grateful. I am wise. I am health. I am happiness. And do not forget to say thank you. Be gracious as if you have already received it. Never pray in supplication, pray in appreciation.

Today.

Today, I am thankful... for each and every day. I will be better every day. I will do more every day. I will greet each day with laughter, love, and gratitude, and say goodnight with a brief reflection of the day's events before I honor my creator for the gift of today. This day was given to me, and should not be taken for granted. I need to concentrate on living in the now, but I will momentarily reflect on the day's events for the sole purpose of seeing what I can improve upon before the sun rises tomorrow and my eyes close tonight. When given the choice to do nothing and take action, I will forever choose to take action. The person who used to do nothing is gone. If this person reappears, I will become aware, take action against them, forgive myself, and move on. TODAY, I TAKE ACTION.

Today, I will become wiser. I will choose to absorb knowledge and educate myself in every subject matter possible, as my thirst for wisdom is a primary driver in my success and freedom. I will condition my body and eternal spirit to make peace with the only enemy I thought I had... my mind. I have spent far too long fighting what I thought was a never ending battle, but not anymore. It is impossible to defeat an enemy that only exists within me. I have no enemies... I have no failures... only opportunities for growth and expansion. TODAY, I GROW. TODAY, I EXPAND. TODAY, I AM WISER.

Today, I will win. Tomorrow I will win. For the rest of my life, I will win. I will be successful. I will be great. My rewards and wealth are a byproduct of the value and service I offer those around me, including myself. The lives I change are my true reward... My success is a byproduct of the lives I change, as well as my decision to change myself. My life is my reward. TODAY, I AM SUCCESSFUL. TODAY, I AM GREAT. TODAY, I WIN.

Today, I overcome. I shall suffer no longer. I will not waste my energy on long-term goals. I will break my long-term goals down into simple daily steps, and instead, devote my energy to becoming the person I must become to reach my long-term goals. Yesterday, I was not that person. Today, I am that person. I am stronger than yesterday; mentally, physically, emotionally, and spiritually. I have not only adapted to, but have overcome the thief that robbed me of fulfilling my destiny yesterday... my mind. TODAY, I AM STRONGER. TODAY, I OVERCOME.

Today, there is no enemy. Today, there is no fear. Not anymore. I am the only thing that has ever stopped me, but today, I forgive myself. I forgive everyone I feel has ever done me wrong, simply because, no one has ever done me wrong. At the time they performed actions which I thought were against me, or wrong, I did not understand myself the way I do now. I can show them compassion, pray for their healing, and hope one day we can sit side by side while I share with them how grateful I am for every breath they take. TODAY, I FORGIVE.

Today, I un-focus. Sometimes people will focus their anger towards me, but I will not focus my anger towards them. I am in control of my feelings, my emotions, and my actions. Only I can make the choice to become upset or angry, and I no longer make that choice. I forgive them. I forgive myself. Pain is necessary, but my suffering is optional. Today I make the decision to never suffer again. TODAY, I AM IN CONTROL.

Today, I realize my purpose. My body belongs to me and so does my mind. And now, I am now in control. This magnificent and beautiful vessel was created for one thing and one thing only... my purpose that God has given me. My destiny that I now realize. It is said that the two most important days of our lives are the day we are born, and the day we realize WHY we were born. For me, that day is today. TODAY, I AM MY PURPOSE.

Today, I make the decision to be wealthy. I make the decision to be healthy. I make the decision to be successful. I make the decision to have a smile on my face even when no one else is smiling. I make the decision to provide for those who cannot provide for themselves. I make the decision to stay in control of my mind. I make the decision to forgive even when I am not forgiven. Today is my purpose. Today is my gift. Today, I am in control. TODAY, IS MY GIFT. TODAY, I TAKE RESPONSIBILITY FOR MY LIFE.

Today, God will move mountains for me, because today, I will move mountains for God. TODAY, I AM READY.

Chapter 10
The Startup Survival Guide

So, the book is over. You can close it if you want. If you do decide to stay, I included The Startup Survival Guide... which is just a book of principles I have been working on and updating. And of course, I provided Today at the end, so you can read it one more time before you put this thing on the shelf. Maybe, you can "pass the book" to someone? Give it a shot. Enjoy my app by the way. I built it for YOU and YOUR freedom:

I have spent so much time writing and delegating over the last year or so, that I almost completely lost sight of just how huge my brand and businesses have become. From the outside it may seem like my life is full of rainbows and jelly beans, but there is a constant gnawing and pulling at my inner being. There are times when I cannot eat, sleep, leave the house, drink water, or conjure up the strength to scratch my nose. There are unanswered questions, never-ending to-do lists, and thousands of unanswered calls and emails tugging at my pant leg every time I take a moment to breathe. This folks, is the life of an entrepreneur. But not just the average entrepreneur—an entrepreneur that is developing a global brand and empire.

The clock says 3AM, and I cannot remember if I woke up early or just haven't been to sleep. All I know is, days of the week no longer matter to me, my legacy does. But I need help... I need an answer. What can I do right now to stay productive? Here is a notepad—that is a good start. Now, what do I write? What if... what if I could come up with a checklist of 5 to 8 questions... hmm – questions? Steps? Things...? Help me out guys, I am not sure how to word it... a list of survival rules for a guy like me...? Not just a guy with a small business, but a guy building a kick ass global empire.

Anyway, as I began making this list, I figured it would make a great chapter to a book, but as the list grew to 12, 15, then 20 items and beyond, I figured it may make a good little publication on its own. Hell, after constantly adding to and updating the content, a couple of years from now, it could very well be a list of 100 principles, with its own hardcover edition. Yes!! Principles!! That is what I will call them!

So, I give you, "The Startup Survival Guide: An ongoing list of necessary principles for someone building a bad ass global empire." The title may change one day, but for right now, I am standing by this one. ☺

I didn't want to create an extravagant list of any sort, nothing above conventional. Nothing with a "WOW" factor. Nothing over the top. Just some common sense factors I did not take into account when I started building my global empire; covering topics I wish someone had covered with me so I could have saved myself thousands of dollars' worth of mistakes, as well as cherished time I will never get back. Take these principles with a grain of salt. Some of them may resonate with you, some may not. But I can promise you, I really wish I had read these in a book when starting my own entrepreneurial journey.

Welcome to the ever-expanding list of my own personal business principles. I promise to give you a list of 100 someday.

1. Your business will only grow as large as your thinking.

There are so many bumper sticker quotes I can think of right now which would make great analogies for this particular topic, but a very relatable one would be, "Whether you think you can, or think you can't -- you are right."

Or thoughts dominate our reality, and whatever we are striving to reach, we very well can and will reach it if we put forth the effort it will take to reach it. Most of the time, that has a lot less to do with performing physical actions as it does with becoming the person needed to fulfill your ultimate desires. Even if there is drastic action that needs to be taken, trying to take that action without changing you think will just leave you sitting on the curb, throwing rocks, and wondering why another entrepreneurial endeavor failed.

Henry Ford was the man who said the quote I listed above. Ford did not just want to build a tiny car company—he wanted to make the first car that would be affordable to the entire population. He also wanted to build an assembly line that could pop those puppies out around the clock. In the fall of 1908, the first Model T left the production plant with a multi-faceted assembly line that could assemble a brand new Model T in just 24 seconds. Whether he had set out to build 10 cars a year, or hundreds per day, he was right. And you can be too. The time is going to pass anyway. You may as well think HUGE and KICK ASS doing it!

2. If you wouldn't, don't expect them to...

In the beginning stages of running my investment firm back in 2014, I came across a lot of "great" ideas. A ton of inventors with contraptions aimed at changing the planet or the way we wash our socks. I met all sorts of artists who never let anyone else see or hear their work before asking for a million dollars to market it. I saw Power Point presentation after Power Point presentation about gadgets and gizmos of plenty, and who's-its and what's-its galore... and if you wanted thing-a-ma-bobs, they had plenty. And they always wanted more and more money. Countless people would come to us with an idea written on paper, and ask for hundreds of thousands, if not millions, of dollars.

In the early stages of the company, we were trying to get capital for everyone who came to us, but we noticed a trend: an approval rating of less than 5%. Why? Because we never took the time to see if their product, plan, or service held any weight. With no sweat equity, effort, or their own capital thrown into a project, how would they expect anyone else to front them any cash? Sadly, they did. But it pushed me to the point to where I would simply ask my potential clients, "How much have you invested in your project?"

This principle does not just apply to investing either. Ask yourself if you would purchase your product. Ask yourself if you would pay for your service. Look at your value proposition from someone else's perspective, or do your best to get genuine feedback from a test group of people. Whether it has to do with purchasing or investing, if you wouldn't, don't expect them to.

3. Focus on building your name more than any product or service.

After being in network-marketing for quite some time, helping people build their own teams of asset and building my own brands, I have learned a valuable fact: no matter what you have to sell, provide, or hold someone's hand into doing, if you have a name for yourself, your job is done. And you don't build a name for yourself overnight. You must give back to your customers, your community, or all of humanity – it just depends on how large your goals are and what your purpose is on this planet. No one cares about your sales script, they want to know that you give a damn about their needs.

"To-do" lists are not as important as affirmation and manifestation practices, consciously changing habits and making better decisions for your future, or assuring yourself of your worthiness to achieve your desires. You must realize though, achieving those desires depends on who YOU are. People follow people, not products. Who are you? How do people see you? Do you wow people enough to desire an association with you, or do you push people away with your negative outlook on life; or forceful sales tactics? People should expect nothing out of you except greatness. You should be known for your ambition, honesty, drive, creativity, and everything you have done to actively progress the planet.

4. Relationships will make or break you.

I have had just as many business partners steal from me and stab me in the back as I have had intimate partners from former relationships. While luckily that number is very few, it still sucks when someone makes conscious decisions to hurt you or doesn't care about your future or well-being.

You are in the big leagues now, which means, you have to start being more conscious of who you associate with. Once you have started making genuine profits, it is time to consider doing full background checks on anyone you know on a personal level. Hang out with the person, learn their habits, hobbies, and how they speak about themselves and other people. By person, I mean: you exchange money, products, or services with them; you bring them on board as a business partner; or you bring them into your life as a social partner. It is important to know who you are dealing with. And while I may have an advantage in knowing a little bit more about behavior than the average bear, it does not stop other people from changing their minds, or even being a really good liar or manipulator. Even I get fooled sometimes or thrown off by ignoring my intuition.

When it comes to "building a legacy," you have to think above and beyond your typical 9-5, mid five-figure a year position, and start thinking about what you can build with a person *and* what they can destroy or take from you. Emotions need to take the backseat on this ride. I do my best to believe in people—but I only let them close to me, personally or business-wise, once I know their potential, capabilities, and ultimate intentions. Sometimes you have to pull up your "big-kid" pants and pass up emotional and bodily urges to achieve your goals. Never lose sight of the bigger picture. It also helps to keep the big picture in mind every step of the way. Making better decisions about who you associate with will just be another byproduct of your winning attitude and success. Partner with the best people, and you will have the best—anything you want.

5. Build a lifestyle, not a business.

If you set out to be self-employed, you can do it. If you set out to own a small business, you can do it. If you set out to own a very large franchise, you can do it. Yes, you really can do any and everything you set your mind to, as long as you are willing to become the person it takes to achieve those goals, and perform the necessary action as well. Never forget that you have to follow all of those silly laws of nature, the universe, God, physics... whatever name you choose to associate with a force beyond your control.

(You can read about those laws to which I am referring by checking out *Breaking Point Better Edition* or *Breaking Laws of Attraction Better Edition*.)

Think about the bigger picture for a minute. Whatever you are doing for income, do you really want to be doing it? Or would you prefer to make yourself some sort of automated system to create wealth? I don't know about you, but I would much rather build a business around my desire to raise and homeschool my daughter, travel, and have the freedom and money to create as many memorable experiences as I possibly can. For my daughter more than myself. This starts with making the decision to build a way of life. Don't just build a business. Decide who you want to be, where you want to go, and what you want to do, *then* figure out how to make income around it.

6. Don't write a book, unless...

When I first started my publishing company, I started it with the intention of recreating for entrepreneurs the boost I received when I wrote my first book. I immediately saw the benefits of becoming an expert or an authority figure in your field, as I was spending a significant amount of time at networking events when my first book launched. Since being an "author" made my business card and resume look more professional, I decided to build my company strictly for entrepreneurs with the same goal. Later, after making the decision to become a genuine content creator, I changed the focus of my publishing company. Rather than helping entrepreneurs write their first books, I decided we would help anyone launch and market a self-published book with us. Having taken the time to publish multiple manuscripts, audio, video, children's books, etc., I have learned the hassles firsthand of how difficult it can be to find good editors, cover creators, publicists, and people who can genuinely help you market a brand.

The entire reason I started the Legacy Status Systems brand was to build an exclusive network of entrepreneurs who wanted to build global empires, rather than just building a small business. I have been a small business owner (there is nothing wrong with being a small business owner), but I hit a point where I wanted to build something bigger for myself and my daughter – and any other family I could possibly have in the future. Regardless of any of the companies I start or become a part of, intellectual property is of great importance to me now. I do not just want to write books;, I want to make comics, illustrated stories, music, movies, software, and any other medium I can use to spread my voice, ideas, and creativity to the world. I learned from the great `Stan Lee, after trying to sell his first few comics and getting nowhere fast, he then decided to concentrate on creating more content. It was only a matter of time before he struck gold and Marvel Comics became the household name it is today. While I said I was not going to place a part of Breaking Bad in this book... I think I may have lied, because these few paragraphs resonate with the message I have written here. Be right back:

I don't know if you are aware of this, but there are a lot of new "authors" out there publishing eBooks like business cards, with hopes to increase their web presence and sales base, and to also give themselves the title of "author." I know, I was one of them... but I learned by living – and living taught me, being an author does not make you a true writer. Practice and perfecting your craft can make you a true writer – just like a drummer, or an air conditioning technician, or a painter...

To all of those authors who are writing books to market yourselves, whether you are paying someone to write your 3,000 word eBook or not, you are falling into a trap. With self-publishing being so easy, and droves of entrepreneurs seeing the benefit(s) in having a book to their name, we are essentially creating the next generation of writers. Authors will be faced with a few choices; do they become one hit wonders who publish a document for a more dynamic business card? Will they ever sell any considerable amount of publications in the course of their lifetime, or own a small eBook that just fades into the background? Do they become one of the many authors who never take the time to learn the art of writing, speaking, and communicating... or, do they become the Joe Gores, Stephen King, Robert Crais, and JK Rowling of tomorrow? (I guess you can tell which writers I admired growing up.) Regardless which path is chosen, I would make one solid recommendation; go back to your original manuscript, even if you have only written one, and rewrite it from your heart. Then, get it printed, no matter how big or small it is. Holding my first book in my hand brought forth almost as much emotion as holding Emma for the first time.

Taking the time to bring anything of substance into the world can drive us straight to a path to greatness, if we allow it. Sharing ourselves with the people of the planet is exactly why we are here. So share.

I decided, I am a writer. I not only want to continue sharing my stories and perspective, I want my readers to feel, hear, and dive into the passion I pour into my writing. I want to be a household name, with a library of well over 200 books written... and that does not include documentaries, seminars, or the audio presentations I am publishing now. I want to leave a legacy for my family... to make the "Criddle" name mean something. I want to be President of the United States, and show my generation what we can achieve when we pour all of our effort into actually completing something. I want to be responsible for the Global Awakening. I want to leave my mark, so the world will know I cared enough to change myself, to in turn become the right person the planet needed for salvation. – Breaking Bad

Don't write a book unless you are planning to do something with it. When I wrote my first book, I had already planned my first 3. There was always a bigger plan to spread a bigger message. Puffing up your business card with a single book and no desire to "change" anything will just raise a whole lot of questions you may not be willing to answer. Be a content creator. DO SOMETHING with your work—don't just write a book because you think it will make you look better.

7. This is your legacy. Are you doing enough?

About 2 years ago, I created a habit of asking myself, "What should you be doing right now?" It was my way of analyzing my surroundings. Activating the "camera" I have mentioned in the past that follows you throughout the day so you can review the footage at the end of the day. When I ask myself what I should be doing, I can immediately ground myself in the moment, and take a 3rd party perspective of the events taking place in my surroundings. Once I gather a full grasp on my very own actions, I decide whether or not I can be doing something to better myself in any way. If there is something I can be working on that will help build my legacy, I jump on it.

I came up with this little analogy the other day while on a radio show: I said, "If you want to be in a strong relationship, you have to become a strong person first."

So many people have this expectation of someone significant coming into their lives and changing everything for them. Unless you are doing work to change your own future, nothing will change. Now, that does not mean hardships, 20 hour days, and drawing blood, it just means you need to be doing something worthy of building a legacy. If you are not building assets, you are wasting your time.

I used to wonder what the difference between wealth and riches were... then I experienced it. Riches are money. Wealthy is what is left when there is no money... or the byproduct of the money. The "who" and "what" you have become. The "where" you live. The "how" you got to that point. Far too many people focus on making money, when they should focus on giving value to others.

There is an entire truckload of wealth and riches just around the corner, waiting for you. Yes, you. What are you going to do to get it here, and what are you going to do to help it show up on your doorstep? Rather than worrying about making money, you should be thinking about how you can make other people money. How can you enrich other's lives? What, of yourself, can you offer to the world to make them change the entire way they live and experience the world? This is your path to riches.

Steve Jobs did it. Mark Cuban did it. Einstein did it. Edison did it. Whether they were rich or wealthy, you know of their names because of the actions they took and the decisions they made that changed your life, not theirs. The most successful and wealthy people to ever walk this earth created their own careers. So, what are you doing? Are you trying to become a member of society? Or are you trying to become your best self?

If you are focusing on trying to build a career with a title that a million other people share; if you are trying to pass a course with fifty other people in your class, with another class of fifty waiting to walk in after you, while that class is being taken in a thousand schools all across the country, be prepared and stop to look around – because there is your competition right there - waiting for you to fuck up so they can snatch the rug right out from underneath you.

But what about you? Your beautiful self? What about the God that God put within you? What about the drive and passion that you have... the gift that NO ONE on this planet has except you? You know it's in you. You were doing it yesterday. You were complimented on it just last week. This morning, someone told you how great you were at it. And tomorrow, someone will tell you that you should do it for a living. So, why aren't you doing it?

Are you afraid? Is your amygdala causing a little too much fear? Is a little too much cortisol seeping into your bloodstream because of your unfamiliarity with the unknown? Are your friends laughing at you and telling you that it's a stupid idea and you shouldn't do it? Did you try it before for a few months, and you were too damn patient to see it through?

Your way to wealth is to provide value to others. The law of compensation. A little law that I have written about many times which states your will be compensated for the amount of value you bring to the world around you. Money and wealth is the byproduct of your value. A byproduct of your service and contribution. This doesn't mean you have to work your ass off doing something you hate. As a matter of fact, your passion should be the exact opposite. You should not only love what you are doing to become wealthy, but you should want to teach others to do it, pay others to let you do it, and be willing to die happily while you are doing it. Your path to wealth creation exists within you. All you have to do is make the

decision to become the "you" that God put you here for. —
Understanding the God Theory

8. Do something publicity worthy.

While a lot of spend ample amounts of money on SEO, advertising, and marketing, all of those efforts will eventually die in vain if someone has not taken the time to build a name for themselves. Most small business owners will open up a store, an office, or start a home-based business and follow all of the same step their competition did when setting up shop. The saddest part is, in a lot of cases, their competition has not achieved the milestones they set out to achieve originally. "The blind leading the blind," as the old saying goes.

If you are concentrating on building your name and fulfilling your purpose, some part of what you are doing should make an impact worthy of gaining some publicity and attention. If someone frowns upon your desire to gather some limelight, they may not align with your purpose, and you may seriously need to reconsider having them in your life. Don't do something outstanding or courageous *just* for publicity—it will never work. If you are performing genuine acts of kindness and gratitude, with a true desire to change our planet for the better, your efforts will be rewarded in due time.

9. Get a mentor, or become a mentor.

While some coaches stand firmly behind the idea of finding a mentor, I do not necessarily think one is needed in all cases. There is this saying that goes something like, "Find someone doing what you want to do, follow them, and become successful."

I stand behind the idea that one should realize no one on the planet can do what you can do. Follow your own purpose and passion, then become successful. And while some people are fortunate enough to have access to people who could potentially be mentors, there are others who would rather be the pioneers and explorers of our premature, enlightened future. I do not want to teach others to do what I have done—I want to teach others that they have the power within them to do whatever they want to do. I want to teach others how to build wealth and a free lifestyle based on their dreams, not the dreams of others.

If you do decide you want a mentor, do not ask someone to be your mentor; become a servant and absorb information as you go along. If you do not have access to a mentor, become the badass that God put you here to be.

10.   Build something profitable, make it sustainable, and then repeat the process.

I see way too many entrepreneurs fall into one of the very same traps I did, which is jumping from one idea to the next, especially when there is not an immediate payoff from the minimal amount of effort put in. I am not saying some people are not putting in enough effort to see a project through, but for too many times, I have watched someone try to build something for a few weeks, or even a few months, then give up and move onto another project, just to repeat the process.

Of course you have to do what it takes to bring in income and pay the bills, but you have to remember, the bigger your dreams are, the more steps it will take to build a foundation. I purchased the first Legacy Status domain almost 3 years ago, and it is just now getting to the point to where it makes sense. I went through countless sales people, friends who needed jobs, and dozens of NDA's signed; with no real long term success. Persistence and perseverance helped me to bring my dream to life. So many people dream of building their legacy too, but give up long before they ever get close. It doesn't have to be hard or take a lot of work, but it sure will be different. Do yourself a favor, stick to a project until it becomes profitable, make it profitable long term, and THEN move onto the next project.

11. Become a dominant force before you have competition, or take yourself out of the "competition zone."

What can one do to combat competition? Well, that is easy: build a name for yourself. Become an idea, not just a business owner. Go beyond SEO and marketing campaigns. Hustle until you never have to introduce yourself again. If you work to become recognizable in an endless sea of faces, you will automatically stand apart from the crowd. It takes so little effort to be just like everyone else, so put forth as much effort as possible, and completely rid yourself of any competition.

12. Everything unfolds like it should, based on your thoughts and actions. The universe will only bring you what you can handle, have handled, or need to grow to handle later.

If you have not yet read *How Can I*, you should seriously consider it, because Josh's book speaks volumes about this very topic. As many times as Emma has begged me for a pet horse, I still haven't gotten her one, and I cannot imagine doing so in the near future. Why? Because I do not believe she can handle the responsibility yet. She would have to prove herself worthy of taking on such an incredibly daunting task. Perhaps one day, we can start with a fish, or even a puppy, but it would not be very responsible of me to burden her with so much hard work, especially when I know she is not ready for it.

The universe acts the same way. You don't have to reach some farfetched pinnacle of success before fame, fortune, and riches come knocking at your door, but you sure have to start working towards it. While we often hear of people winning the lottery, or coming across great sums of money just to end up broker than they were before, I have learned to find solace in the struggle. If at any moment, I feel even the slightest hint of dissatisfaction with where my life is, or where it is heading, I remember: it is my fault. Rather than becoming angry or upset about my lack of achievement, I come to terms with the reality of the situation, and start making a game plan to tackle the particulars I need to change about myself.

Unfortunately, this simple action is rarely performed by the average person, if ever. So, if you ever find yourself frustrated about the lack of growth or progress in your reality, remember, the universe will only deliver what you can handle. If you want to handle more, then DO more.

13. Always have income.

I think this goes without saying, but you should always have income flowing in. If you are working at a job, do not jump ship just yet. Life becomes a whole lot easier if you can create enough income to replace the 9-to-5 paycheck you are receiving now. Do not put yourself in a situation where you panic about where your next dollar or next meal will come from. This state of survival mode will cause you to make decisions that could very well be detrimental to your future, rather than helpful.

Find simple ways to bring in income if you absolutely refuse, or lack the means to work a "typical" job. There are plenty of freelancing websites online for people with all sorts of skills. Nonprofit organizations are hidden gems for people who could be looking to make some extra income. While there is quite a bit of volunteer work to be had, there are plenty of other perks and opportunities that come along with volunteering your time instead of sitting on your butt. If you don't have a lot of money to invest, start working on building assets through network-marketing or your first pieces of intellectual property. Building leverage is key to building wealth, and passive income.

14. Many of the problems you feel are holding your business at bay were problems long before you had a business. The problem isn't the business – the problem is you.

There are so many of us who want to succeed, but we are not willing to do what it takes to get there. And, what it takes to get there isn't always about tasks or to-do lists. Success comes from the person. As Bob Proctor says, "It is not about making a million dollars. It is about the person you become on the way to making a million dollars." I am paraphrasing of course, but you get the idea.

While so many of us will quickly blame other people in our lives, and not take responsibility for our actions, the ones who succeed are the ones who are willing to own up to their mistakes *and* stop performing the repetitive and sometimes addictive behaviors that have been holding them at bay.

While there are often extenuating circumstances, most of the errors and lack of accomplishments that I have experienced were directly correlated to the actions I did not take. This stems from not becoming the person I needed to be to achieve those goals. Today has been a spectacular day: I have written and edited more than 6,000 words. Could you imagine how much content I would have written if I wrote 6,000 words every day? But I don't. Why? Because I have not become that person yet. That is only one example—I have a million bajillion things I have to work on myself, but I do realize, I am the one holding back my own success. As I have said before, "Your success is solely dependent upon the second letter in success."

15. Network-Marketing is a good tool to keep in your arsenal.

Everyone is looking for an inexpensive business to invest in, but everyone will talk trash about multi-level marketing. While broke people allow themselves to exist within a paradigm of "pyramid scheme" this and "scam" that, there is a small group of people out there putting forth a tremendous amount of effort into their network marketing companies. This group of people generally consists of 3 different types of network-marketers:

I. The beginners who live on the hype and draw of the company. Because these people take their company's message seriously, they may actually hit it big by proxy, or because an upline decides to hold their hand due to genuine effort or success.

2. The people who signed up to shut someone up, or they don't care enough to ever build the business. You will meet a whole slew of these people in the network-marketing business. And these are usually the people who speak the most negativity towards companies that "never worked."

3. The affluent. The popular. The well connected. These people do great in network-marketing by default because they have already built a following, a brand, a company, etc. There is something they have accomplished which makes network-marketing look easy from the outside. And do you know why it is easy for them now? Because they probably put forth a whole bunch of effort a long time ago. They deserve respect, regardless of how easy you think you have it.

Regardless of what network-marketing company you get yourself involved in, there are not many other inexpensive, established businesses you can invest in with such a high potential return. Your effort in network-marketing depends solely upon the amount of effort you are willing to put into building your name, not your network-marketing business.

16.   Find people who believe in your purpose.

I wanted to take "relationships" a step further and touch more on the types of people you need to surround yourself with. You need people who are on your team. Period. You do not always need a bunch of "yes" men around you either. It is crucial to have members within your entourage who will offer constructive criticism just as much as offering support to help you along your purpose. I do not think people who do not fit in this criteria are not a necessary part of our life; we will always have people in our lives who could care less, people who do not like us, people who do not know we exist... the list goes on and on. The important thing is to be weary of those you allow in your close inner circle. If they are not on your team, they are a waste of your time.

17.   Be ready for the explosion of abundance.

I meet so many people who say they want to be rich, but they do not put forth the necessary effort. That is why less than 5% of the population could be considered rich. The other 95% tell themselves lies about why they are not rich in an attempt to make themselves feel better about not doing what it takes. If someone were to come to me and needed a solution to make an extra ten or twenty thousand dollars in the next 12 months, there would be thousands, if not millions of options available to us. If someone were to come to me and needed a solution to make an extra million dollars in the next 12 months, suddenly we are faced with much fewer options that will require an approach beyond the subtleties of a five figure a year income. Unless this person already possessed the knowledge to make this kind of income, meaning, they had done it before.

The truth is, if you are going to build an empire, you have to be willing to build the foundation of an empire. When I wrote my first book, I instantly learned the power of having my first asset. Then came a second, and a third. Then I started a publishing company so I could not only help other writers publish their work, but I would also get my hands on more assets. A foundation is built stone by stone, brick by brick. There are so many pieces to the "get rich" puzzle, and one of those pieces is your first asset. Then the next and the next. You have to continue to build assets, or build a foundation whether you are in real estate, business investments, stocks, or intellectual property. There are not many "jobs" you can do that will land you in any sort of "rich" category.

You need leverage. Leverage comes from taking what you have and doing as much as you can with it. The more you have, the more you can do with it. This is why you constantly need to be creating content, building a name for yourself, building an entourage of good people, and working towards the big picture. Wealth is what you are left with when the money is gone, and no one can take wealth away from you. Wealth brings you abundance, and when the world learns who you are, you need to be ready for them. If you have nothing for them to buy, you will miss a crucial piece to the "get rich" puzzle.

18. "Don't play football if you are not willing to tackle someone." – Greg Doss

When I was going through my custody battle, a buddy of mine told me the quote above. Not only was he a radio host and a constitutional law expert, he was also a little league football coach. On the first day of practice, he would lay down his rules and expectations he had for and of his players. One of those expectations was tackling. Not just to be tackled, but to get tackled.

I think a lot of us business owners are willing to get tackled; some are even willing to get back up. Society teaches us to persevere, but no one has really taught us to attack. Why build a company with a strong defensive plan and exit strategy when you can build a company that will completely blow your competition out of the water? Instead of trying to improve upon the things your competition is doing, why don't you instead find out what your competition is not doing, or would never think of doing?

19.   Are you really an entrepreneur? Or do you just own a job?

Entrepreneur is such a fun word, and often misused too. While the average "job" owner will call themselves an entrepreneur, I like to think of its true meaning as being a little closer to the dictionary definition; an entrepreneur manages multiple projects while making above-average risks. I would also like to throw in there, an entrepreneur typically understands the importance of an asset, and works towards building assets, rather than bringing in immediate income.

A plumber is not an entrepreneur; the owner of a plumbing company with many contractors, assets, equipment, and cash flow is an entrepreneur. A doctor is not an entrepreneur; the guy who spent zero time in medical school and owns the hospital where the doctor practices medicine is an entrepreneur. A young lady who quits her job to become a maid is not an entrepreneur. Sadly, she needs people making money for her before she can consider herself an entrepreneur.

Remember, there is nothing wrong with being a small business or job owner, just make sure you know what an entrepreneur is before you start calling yourself one.

"The average job, which accounts for a majority of the populous, has a starting point where the result is already placed in front of the employee. They are then taught how to mimic the result. This behavior then produces thoughts in the subconscious mind, which produce feelings about the thought. These feelings drive the person into action. These actions cycle back to the original result. This behavior is continually repeated until the mind is forced to revert back to the original cycle, rather than finding innovative solutions to

create a better result, the mind is motivated to repeat the same behavior.

When people have the ability to choose or create certain results for themselves, they are forced to come up with an idea. The idea then produces thoughts, which create feelings of emotion about the idea. Those feelings then drive them into action. These actions produce their very own result, based upon their original creative idea. Rather than being told to mimic the result from the beginning, this cycle reverts back to the creation of more ideas, be it innovation, or entirely new paths to explore." – Trainer to Trillionaire

20. The best sales person does not have to sell anything.

I remember when I first got into network-marketing. I do not mean to talk about it so much, but it was kind of my gateway drug into assets, wealth, vision boards, and manifestation. Network-marketing helped me believe I really could become rich and afford all of the subtleties of life only a select few enjoy. Once I started thinking big, I never looked back.

I realized, I could talk anyone into network-marketing, regardless of what company I was involved with. But it never had to do with the company, it had to do with the beliefs the people had in me. Were it not for my desire to educate myself, make real changes in my community, and actively take steps to become a better human being, I would not be the person I am today. And the person I am today doesn't have to sell anything. I rarely even have to show up anymore. People know that when my name or my brands are involved, value comes along without question. I have worked diligently to construct a brand name within myself, and because of that hard work, I no longer have to sell anything.

21.   Life will always happen. Don't let it get in the way.

You are not just waking up and giving it your all so you can be the absolute best—you are giving it your all so you can be the absolute best on even your worst day. Some people believe I stay positive *all* the time. They think I never have bad days or upset feelings. This is not true. I do have bad days. I too live with daily frustrating situations. But I also realize, there is a time to be frustrated. Just as there is a time to be angry, impatient, or sad. Ignoring these feelings and emotions does nothing for us, except cause our body to operate in a deficit or a mindset of resistance—it is nearly impossible to "not think" about something by ignoring it. During those times of frustration, embrace your emotions, confront the problem, and find the quickest solution necessary to regain peace of mind.

Allow yourself to have a minute, an hour, or even a day to "feel bad," and remember, it is just a feeling. Saying "I am" only causes you to identify with a problem, which in turn causes the pain or emotion you are feeling to become a permanent part of your being. Saying "I feel" allows your body and mind to still feel empowered, even when life is doing something you might not particularly like. Remember: pain is necessary, but suffering is optional. We suffer when we put ourselves in a deficit or in a mindset of resistance. Let life happen, and do your best to stay in control. It will be much easier to dust yourself off once you realize this simple fact: Life really does go on.

22. If you are not prepared to fail, you are not prepared to succeed.

In principle number 19, I mentioned a behavior cycle I came up with for *Trainer to Trillionaire*. While there are a lot of us who want to succeed in creating a gigantic business, we must prepare ourselves for one of the most crucial elements of success. That element, is failure.

While you have been taught your entire life to shy away from making mistakes, fearing the reprisal of an upset teacher, disappointed boss, or misunderstanding spouse, mistakes absolutely must be made in order to reach your goals. Why? Because there is absolutely no way anyone will ever reach their long term goals the first time out. Failing allows us to critique the process, create a better value proposition for our product or service, or move onto a different path entirely. I am not an advocate of giving up on your goals, however, I am an advocate of continually working towards a goal until you are absolutely certain it will not work, then moving on.

Michael Jordan attributes all of the accomplishments he achieved in his lifetime of playing basketball to the sheer volume of failures he experienced. If he had given up on himself after any one single failure, the sport of basketball may be played completely different today. At your typical job these days, a failure can land you a reprimand or even a spot in the unemployment line. In the life of the entrepreneur, you really only have to be "right" once in order to experience the successes you desire.

23. Don't try to do it all on your own— whenever possible, delegate a task.

Being a trainer for quite some time, I met a lot of people who only wanted to work on their strengths. Men who neglected their legs for a more powerful chest would naturally gravitate towards the bench press as I would lead them to the leg press. Women with powerful glutes and hamstrings would head over to the leg press as I would walk them to the bench press to strengthen their upper body. While I spent many years turning "Averages Joes" into competitive athletes by focusing on their weaknesses, the exact opposite holds true when you are dealing with a startup business.

Sadly, I have wasted a great deal of time as an entrepreneur, focusing too much of my time on my weaknesses rather than focusing on my strengths. While I spent a great deal of my life carrying so much pride in my ability to multitask and learn new skills, I have found now, success comes from concentrating on what I am good at, (and hopefully, what you are good at makes money) and paying someone else to do the tasks I don't have time to get to. When I get an idea for a new cd, I gather whatever audio I need to gather, and send it to the studio. When I finish a manuscript, I pass it off to an editor. A year ago I would have purchased an in-home audio studio to learn the art of manipulating sound on my own. As for my manuscripts, I would probably be on the 28th edit of my 3rd book—instead of working on books 14 through 20. Both tasks would have taken a considerable amount of time and energy; effort I could have been applying towards the creation of more content, instead of executing menial tasks I don't have the education to perform.

24.   Be open to any opportunity.

There is more than one way to tie a shoe, skin a cat, and make passive income. I spoke earlier about entrepreneurs who give up on opportunities before they have time to seed, sprout, and grow; that being said, I may have forgotten to mention how good it could be for you to take on a second, third, or even tenth venture.

"Don't put all of your eggs in one basket." Meaning, there is nothing wrong with working towards multiple streams of income at once. Don't stretch yourself so thin that you are losing sleep, sanity, or money, but don't pass up on an opportunity just because it seems like "work." Sometimes, borrowing a little time and energy from one project could very well make giant waves in another. Follow your gut, and if you feel inspired to start on a new opportunity, go for it.

25.   Yes, you should appreciate what you have, but you MUST be hungry for more. Always.

Being grateful plays a major role in starting anything successful. Possessing the ability to give, receive, try, and fail, blah, blah, blah— this is a skill that is not to be taken lightly. Gratitude takes practice, just as mindfulness and awareness do. Far too many of us hold grudges against the world because, "it just isn't fair." Why must everything always be so difficult? We can we not just have the things we want?

I never did understand it when someone told me, "You won't have your dream car until you love and appreciate the car you have." While I can see their point about appreciation, I hardly loved my car. And while I was indeed grateful for having a vehicle to safely

164

transport my daughter and me from point A to point B, I could still be hungry for something better.

We lie to ourselves way too often, telling ourselves we are okay with our small apartment, subpar vehicle, or even our unfulfilling relationships. But we tell ourselves this lie so we can feel better about not doing what it takes to have something better. When the body gets hungry, the mind searches for food—this is the same principle that should be applied to your wealth, brand, and any businesses you have, each and every day. Be grateful for everything you have, but stay hungry. The hunger will keep you on the search for more.

My uncle always told me, "The only thing that happens when you retire, is you die." Sadly, after he retired, he passed on. Why? Because "the search" is what keeps the human alive. Our will to live comes from our desire to grow, and the opposite of growth, is death. If you want to keep growing, you have to keep eating, so stay hungry.

26.   Make reading, relaxation, and exercise a priority, every day.

I am not going to talk about exercise. I have talked about it enough in many of my books. I will say however, make time for the gym. Getting the blood flowing, the heart pumping, and the muscles aching are just as good for business as they are for the heart and brain. Why? Stress and anger elimination, weight loss, increased confidence, increased endorphins and "happy" hormones, boost in brain computing power, sharper memory, better sleep... do I really need to keep going?

The library is free—did you know that? Oh yeah? Then why does less than 3% of the country's population have a library card? Because our education system destroyed what books represent. There hits a point in just about every child's life where they stop looking at a trip to the library as a fun adventure, and start looking at it as a useless chore; just a place to study or kill time on the computer. There are over 130 million books in circulation today, and all of them are waiting to captivate your imagination, teach you how to build a homemade helicopter, or yes, even build a lucrative, multimillion dollar business. But the trick is, you have to read them. Turn off your TV, close out Facebook, and get lost in a real book.

And while you are doing all of that, don't forget to "take a chill pill" (as Emma would say). Have you ever floated a river? It is seriously one of the most fun and relaxing experiences you will ever have. Do you know how to do it? Take a bunch of floats and a bunch of friends to a river, sit down in the floats, and have the time of your life. This steady flow of the water can perfectly describe life's steady flow of abundance. At some point in your life, someone told you that "hard work" was the only way to achieve your goals. Well, since that hasn't worked, try my advice for a little while. Relax. Stop resisting, and let the current carry you to your destiny.

27.   Be as open and transparent as possible.

So many of us are afraid of our competition, but we don't realize, competition is almost non-existent once we make the choice to create something. No one can steal an original idea and you cannot accuse someone of stealing an idea if you decide to do nothing with it. In the early days of Legacy Status Systems, I spent more time having potential sales people read and sign non-disclosure agreements than I ever did training them. I was so worried about someone stealing our "trade secrets," I never took the time to properly motivate my team or give any direction to my contractors. It was only after I "let go" of this mistrust that my business started moving anywhere.

Now, rather than being so secretive, we happily let new contractors, artists, and "Average Joes" take a look at our business model and patented interface system. One of the first tasks my development team performs when bringing a new designer on board is participating in an open forum discussion of where we are, where we want to be, and how we can grow further as a team. There are no trade secrets anymore, and there are even customers we cannot handle either. So what do we do? We share. We share information, we pass on customers, and we make recommendations based on the betterment of everyone involved, not just the company.

Writing books about my life has helped me to become more open and transparent as well. Vulnerability gives you a strength money cannot buy: freedom.

28. You are your only competition—if you make your goals big enough.

I mentioned earlier:

If someone were to come to me and needed a solution to make an extra ten or twenty thousand dollars in the next 12 months, there would be thousands, if not millions of options available to us. If someone were to come to me and needed a solution to make an extra million dollars in the next 12 months, suddenly we are faced with much fewer options that will require an approach beyond the subtleties of a five figure a year income.

For just a moment, imagine society as a pyramid. At the bottom of the pyramid is 99.9% of the population, fighting to achieve average goals and milestones. The further you travel up the top of the pyramid, the lonelier your life becomes. Why? Because there isn't as much competition at the top. There aren't as many people trying to make a billion dollars as there are people trying to make an extra twenty. Action and perseverance will help you achieve your goals, but I must admit, it is rather fun having goals so large that no one can get in my way—except myself of course.

29. Position yourself wisely. There is nothing worse than becoming great at something useless.

John D. Rockefeller had his entire fortune in marine shipping when he caught a glimpse of a train just outside his office window. Even though he had seen the train stopped at the station many times, this particular instance filled his mind and body with a paradigm shift and a whole new manner in which to construct his business. Almost overnight, he pulled all of his money out of shipping and invested everything in the railway system. I know I am skipping a lot of details, but know that this move eventually led to the boom of the railway industry, the automotive industry, the oil industry, and practically every single facet of life we enjoy today.

Mr. Rockefeller positioned himself wisely. In one single glimpse, he saw a whole new way to ship merchandise and travel. Whale oil was being used to keep our homes lit, and boats just couldn't get cargo across the US fast enough, nor could a boat drive right into the center of the country to deliver goods either. Steve Jobs knew that people wanted to "carry 1,000 songs in their pocket," and

Mark Zuckerberg knew people wanted to be "present" on the internet.

In *The Valuation Evaluation*, I discuss the never-ending amount of "great" ideas I came across in the early stages of owning Legacy Status Investments. That said, a lot of the business plans I looked at were a result of bad positioning. There are way too many entrepreneurs focused on "improvement" when we should be focusing on "innovation." We are explorers, not babysitters and caretakers. A good entrepreneur positions himself where the marketplace is making money; a great entrepreneur creates a new marketplace.

30.   Get paid for what you do. Discounts are for people who do not know their worth. Get paid just for being yourself.

Do not offer discounts. Do not devalue yourself. Offering something for free is just silly. If you are offering free products or services to not only fulfill the laws of the universe, but also bring more attention and value to your business, that is one thing… To give someone a price for the position you have allowed yourself to get paid for, and then offer discounts, or devalue yourself, can show a lack of confidence in your ability to lead or direct. Some will say, "Well, I will only discount in the beginning…"

No you won't. You will find yourself in a trap of forever offering discounts to friends, family, associates, etc. Set a price and stick with it. You are worth it. – Trainer to Trillionaire

On a daily basis, I take at least a half hour to myself for affirmations and breathing exercises. This does not coincide with my prayer or meditation because I do believe these are very separate practices. That being said, I do have quite a few mantras that have stuck with me, regardless of how much I feel I've evolved in my life. One of those mantra is: I get paid just for being me.

In my early stages of being a trainer, being a speaker, and even being an author, I would often have to step outside of myself and realize that I AM the reason people respond to me – not my title or my position. When I first came back to Dallas and applied for a position at the big box gym I worked out of, I was actually afraid of being a small fish in a very big pond. I thought my title of "Personal Trainer" increased my value and worth as a person. But I soon realized, I brought value and worth to the industry.

You shouldn't be focused on building a job or a business; you should focus on building yourself. It doesn't matter if you want better friends, better pay, better opportunities, or a better relationship, building your "self" is the only answer.

In closing...

This list will definitely grow. Had I written this manuscript a year ago, it probably would have only consisted of 5 to 8 principles. Not to mention, all of the grammar and syntax errors you would have found throughout the book. I enjoy sharing content and ideas with you. And I really only do it to show others that they can do it to.

You picked up this book because you are interested in building a legacy. Something inside you is screaming for you to wake up and stop living an average, incomplete, and unfulfilled life. You are the only thing that has ever held you back. So, if you are building a global empire, and things get tough, remember: they are supposed to be. Once you made the decision to stop following the crowd, you invited all of those hardships into your life. If building something bigger than yourself was easy, there would just be "the way," and everyone would do it. But there isn't just one way. And if you are reading any of my books, it is because you know you need as much help as you can get. Build yourself a kick ass business, and don't blow your head off along the way.

Today.

Today, I am thankful... for each and every day. I will be better every day. I will do more every day. I will greet each day with laughter, love, and gratitude, and say goodnight with a brief reflection of the day's events before I honor my creator for the gift of today. This day was given to me, and should not be taken for granted. I need to concentrate on living in the now, but I will momentarily reflect on the day's events for the sole purpose of seeing what I can improve upon before the sun rises tomorrow and my eyes close tonight. When given the choice to do nothing and take action, I will forever choose to take action. The person who used to do nothing is gone. If this person reappears, I will become aware, take action against them, forgive myself, and move on. TODAY, I TAKE ACTION.

Today, I will become wiser. I will choose to absorb knowledge and educate myself in every subject matter possible, as my thirst for wisdom is a primary driver in my success and freedom. I will condition my body and eternal spirit to make peace with the only enemy I thought I had... my mind. I have spent far too long fighting what I thought was a never ending battle, but not anymore. It is impossible to defeat an enemy that only exists within me. I have no enemies... I have no failures... only opportunities for growth and expansion. TODAY, I GROW. TODAY, I EXPAND. TODAY, I AM WISER.

Today, I will win. Tomorrow I will win. For the rest of my life, I will win. I will be successful. I will be great. My rewards and wealth are a byproduct of the value and service I offer those around me, including myself. The lives I change are my true reward... My success is a byproduct of the lives I change, as well as my decision to change myself. My life is my reward. TODAY, I AM SUCCESSFUL. TODAY, I AM GREAT. TODAY, I WIN.

Today, I overcome. I shall suffer no longer. I will not waste my energy on long-term goals. I will break my long-term goals down into simple daily steps, and instead, devote my energy to becoming the person I must become to reach my long-term goals. Yesterday, I was not that person. Today, I am that person. I am stronger than yesterday; mentally, physically, emotionally, and spiritually. I have not only adapted to, but have overcome the thief that robbed me of fulfilling my destiny yesterday... my mind. TODAY, I AM STRONGER. TODAY, I OVERCOME.

Today, there is no enemy. Today, there is no fear. Not anymore. I am the only thing that has ever stopped me, but today, I forgive myself. I forgive everyone I feel has ever done me wrong, simply because, no one has ever done me wrong. At the time they performed actions which I thought were against me, or wrong, I did not understand myself the way I do now. I can show them compassion, pray for their healing, and hope one day we can sit side by side while I share with them how grateful I am for every breath they take. TODAY, I FORGIVE.

Today, I un-focus. Sometimes people will focus their anger towards me, but I will not focus my anger towards them. I am in control of my feelings, my emotions, and my actions. Only I can make the choice to become upset or angry, and I no longer make that choice. I forgive them. I forgive myself. Pain is necessary, but my suffering is optional. Today I make the decision to never suffer again. TODAY, I AM IN CONTROL.

Today, I realize my purpose. My body belongs to me and so does my mind. And now, I am now in control. This magnificent and beautiful vessel was created for one thing and one thing only... my purpose that God has given me. My destiny that I now realize. It is said that the two most important days of our lives are the day we are born, and the day we realize WHY we were born. For me, that day is today. TODAY, I AM MY PURPOSE.

Today, I make the decision to be wealthy. I make the decision to be healthy. I make the decision to be successful. I make the decision to have a smile on my face even when no one else is smiling. I make the decision to provide for those who cannot provide for themselves. I make the decision to stay in control of my mind. I make the decision to forgive even when I am not forgiven. Today is my purpose. Today is my gift. Today, I am in control. TODAY, IS MY GIFT. TODAY, I TAKE RESPONSIBILITY FOR MY LIFE.

Today, God will move mountains for me, because today, I will move mountains for God. TODAY, I AM READY.

Um... close the book. Weirdo.

www.ingramcontent.com/pod-product-compliance
Lightning Source LLC
Chambersburg PA
CBHW031049180526
45163CB00002BA/754